T0149408

YOUR PAST IS A GIFT

HOLLIE BELLE

BALBOA.PRESS

A DIVISION OF HAY HOUSE

Balboa Press books may be ordered through booksellers or by contacting:

Balboa Press
A Division of Hay House
1663 Liberty Drive
Bloomington, IN 47403
www.balboapress.com.au
AU TFN: 1 800 844 925 (Toll Free inside Australia)
AU Local: (02) 8310 7086 (+61 2 8310 7086 from outside Australia)

Because of the dynamic nature of the Internet, any web addresses or links contained in this book may have changed since publication and may no longer be valid. The views expressed in this work are solely those of the author and do not necessarily reflect the views of the publisher, and the publisher hereby disclaims any responsibility for them.

The author of this book does not dispense medical advice or prescribe the use of any technique as a form of treatment for physical, emotional, or medical problems without the advice of a physician, either directly or indirectly. The intent of the author is only to offer information of a general nature to help you in your quest for emotional and spiritual well-being. In the event you use any of the information in this book for yourself, which is your constitutional right, the author and the publisher assume no responsibility for your actions.

Any people depicted in stock imagery provided by Getty Images are models, and such images are being used for illustrative purposes only. Certain stock imagery © Getty Images.

Print information available on the last page.

ISBN: 978-1-5043-0701-7 (sc)
ISBN: 978-1-5043-0702-4 (e)

Balboa Press rev. date: 07/29/2024

This book is dedicated to my Wish.

May you find all the answers you will ever need within these pages. This is my way of ensuring that I will always be with you. Even when I am long gone from this Earth and that you may always know who I am.

I want you to know how I feel about you at all times. That I love you more than anything in this world and that I am so thankful that you finally came into our lives. I treasure every minute I get to share with you.

CONTENTS

PREFACE

This book is dedicated to everyone that has touched my life. To my amazing parents. May they know how much I love them and that I am so lucky to have had them as my parents. They have taught me so much about life and themselves, and I am ever so grateful for the time we have had together.

I wish to give thanks to my sister Anna. Without you, my journey could not have been the same, and this book may not have been made. I love you more than you will ever know because, of all the people that have come and gone in my life, you are the one that has shown me *who I am*.

To my cousins who were my source of unconditional love when I was growing up. Words cannot express my love for you. You gave me so much joy, and you taught me that love could be found in all sorts of beautiful places. Thank you.

To my amazing mother-in-law, Emily. You give me inspiration every single day, and I could not have come this far without you. I love you to the ends of the earth and beyond. Thank you for your wisdom and sharing your knowledge with me and for always treating me like the daughter you never had.

To my soul mate Daniel, I can't thank you enough, and I don't know if my awakening would have taken place without you. You are a real gift. Many times I fight you because I'm resisting the change, but you never give up on me... Your insightful views on life have been my catalyst towards my complete clarity. It is almost as if you know me better than I know myself. Thank you. Thank you for pushing me to be the best person I can be. I love you more than you will ever know.

Lastly, I wish to thank Laura, my Wish. You are the source of my inspiration. You remind me every day what is truly important. Helping me follow my joy, my heart, my bliss just by watching you be all of these things. I had forgotten what it was to be alive until you came along. Thank you, my precious girl. Thank you so much. This story exists because of you, my beauty.

This book is dedicated to you my dear friend with the intention that the knowledge contained within these pages, may guide you to let go of your fear and your old beliefs about yourself. May you find the answers that allow you, to be the **you**, you've always dreamed of being. This book is written with all my love for you. Now go, be free.

INTRODUCTION

This book was written through the eyes of a child. My inner child. In the hope that somewhere within these pages, something may resonate with you and help you find your inner child. So that you can give this young individual all the love and care they need.

It is a glimpse into my journey and how my thoughts have created every single experience in my life. I have written my story for you, so that you may understand the moments that you have set up in your life and help you create the life of your dreams. Deliberately and intentionally from now on.

I used to have a recurring dream that I could fly like Peter Pan. It was so vivid. I could feel the breeze on my face. I felt so free. It was wonderful. At some point in my dream, I forget how to fly, and this fills my soul with such sorrow. While we were all born with the power to fly, most of us get lost along the way and forget how to. I'm sure at times you can feel your inner spirit flapping its wings. It is begging you to set it free and let it soar.

My life has been so simple, and yet it is the perfect example of how our thoughts create our reality and how we can spend a whole lifetime missing the point of our existence. How one single event can change how you view the world for most of your life and more importantly how you see yourself.

Throughout the book, you will find what I was thinking at the time and often I will make a comment in italics of my thoughts regarding this moment in my life today.

I invite you to use this book as your journal and take this journey with me. At the end of each chapter, there will be an invitation for you to look at your life so that you can start finding the gift in every moment. Life is giving you each moment as an opportunity that you may *know* who you are. Consequently, everything that comes to you is what you need. Start peeling all the layers of wrapping paper off today and discover what's inside each gift.

I believe with all my heart that until we can make peace with our past and understand the blessing in every moment, we cannot move forward. At each point, we have made interpretations about others, about the world, about ourselves. As children, we take in what adults tell us as true. To be awake to who you truly are is to understand that it was always **their** truth. What they believed about themselves and the world around them.

Understand that an adult who has a heart full of love, cannot harm another human being or living thing. Therefore, if an adult hurt you, physically or emotionally, it was just an expression of the pain they were carrying within them. The pain of feeling unwanted, unloved, unworthy and not good enough. Their anger towards you was never about you and for some adults what they do is all they have ever known. It is up to each one of us to choose whether the cycle of abuse continues.

You are here reading this book because it is your time to be happy. It is your time to make peace with your past. Find the blessings in each and every moment you have experienced. Free yourself from every interpretation you have created that does not serve you. It is your time to release every thought that makes you feel bad about yourself and begin embracing the truth. The truth that you are love. You were born to love and give love and be love. **You are pure love.**

May you *know* at all times that you are loved and have

always been loved. That your light is far more beautiful than the simple exterior, you are looking at with your own eyes. May you always *know* that you are not separate. You are not disconnected. You have never been alone.

It seems like, the times I had felt the loneliest in my life have been when the most people surrounded me. I felt alone due to my view of the world because most of my life had been spent choosing to believe that I was separate. First and foremost, I am separate from God, my creator. Therefore, I am separate from everything else. Something inside of me was telling me that this was not true.

Life becomes an entirely different dance when you *know* you are not separate. Understanding how connected you truly are to everyone and everything. Finding the gift of every moment that you have lived is the only way you will find peace in your mind.

I've made every effort to include the bare minimum of the people that affected my life. Excluding their details is to protect their privacy because this is not their story. **The book you are about to read is my story** and as you follow along you will understand how to write your own story with my book.

The thoughts and ideas I am sharing with you are collective consciousness. They are not my own. They are inside all of us. The idea that we are not alone has always been in the back of your mind. Energy connects all of us. Everything you say and everything you do affects others. Similarly, you are influenced by everyone that you come in contact with every day.

Whether you choose to accept them and believe these are true is entirely up to you. What you believe has always been up to you. All that is genuine and real is inside of you. You just need to *know* it. However, hearing the words and knowing them are two different things. Experience is what takes the words and turns them into knowingness.

Take this journey with me today. Don't put it off for one more second. Fall in love with your life and with who you are. In the beginning, it will feel like hard work, because we are not in the habit of working on ourselves. All of our focus has always been on others. It is time to make it a habit. As a result, you will be in love with the process of learning more and more about yourself.

Otherwise, you will stay on the same path you are already on. Feeling that there is something else out there but not being able to tap into it. Change means doing something different. For this reason, it is imperative that you take the first step. Do the exercises marked out for you in this book. Read over the chapters as many times as you need to. Each time you do, something new will pop up for you revealing something new about who you are.

May this book guide you to your inner peace. May it guide you to your joy and your bliss. Follow each chapter carefully. Look at your own life. Look at what you have created up to this point in your life. I believe that we choose our parents and the environment we come into as it is of the most benefit to our growth. Whether we decide to let our beginnings define us for the rest of our lives is entirely up to us.

WHO DO YOU THINK YOU ARE?

My life ended when I was five years old. At least life as I knew it.

Hi, my name is Hollie, and I was the firstborn child. I was born in Adelaide, Australia. My parents were immigrants who had traveled from Argentina in search of a better life for their family. I was named after my neighbor. She was a lovely English lady. My parents just found her name so different from all the Spanish names they knew. I guess they wanted me to have a unique name.

Apparently, I had hair all over my body when I was born. It was so rare that the nurses kept coming up to the window to look at me. All of the other babies were fair and with very sparse hair. Some had no hair at all. I even had hair on my face. My Dad said that I looked so much like a monkey, that it made my Mom cry. Great! I'd barely been in the world for a few hours and already was making an impact.

I came into the world just two years after they arrived in Australia, so it was a very stressful time for them. My parents were in a foreign country, learning a foreign language with a newborn baby.

With no money in their pockets, they had taken the plunge and decided to try a new place. That was why they came to

Australia. Mom and Dad came all this way in the hope that they could give us, their children, everything we could ever need or want.

My dad was the youngest of eleven children. He was born on a farm, and life there was very rough. As Dad was needed to help with all the work on the farm from quite a young age, he wasn't able to complete primary school. School was not a vital part of survival in my dad's childhood. Dad's parents did not display any signs of love or affection towards him because it was regarded as a sign of weakness. And boys especially had to be strong. If Dad was "naughty" or did something "wrong," he copped quite severe beatings from his father.

My Grandfather used his belt to hit Dad. He hit my dad until his arm was tired and he was unable to strike him with the belt anymore. It was the same for all the siblings. The older siblings were resentful of, the younger ones because, by the time they were born, my Grandfather was more elderly and wasn't able to punish the younger brothers as severely as he had punished them.

These beatings would leave my dad bedridden for two to three days at a time. It was considered the only way to ensure that your children would be good, honest citizens in society. The fear of raising thieves, murderers, or rapists was too high. That was the ultimate sign that you had not done a good job with your children. You had been too soft on them. It was the worst thing that could happen to you. The point was to make the child too afraid to commit the same mistake again. If the punishment were harsh enough, the child would remember and not repeat that mistake.

Both of my Mom's parents died when she was five years old. They perished in an accident at a very young age. So one of my Mom's aunts, adopted my Mom and her two sisters, even though she had six children of her own. This aunt felt that my Mom was a burden. An extra strain financially and was an extra mouth to feed. Mom had to start working at a very young age to help put food on the table. Having to work at such an early age meant that she didn't get to finish primary school, which was a shame because she loved learning. For being disobedient, my Mom was punished with severe beatings as well. For my parents, this was a normal childhood, where hunger and extreme physical violence were a way of life.

In truth, my Mom and I had one thing in common. Something happened to us at the age of five that would change the way we viewed the world and life itself. It's nice to know we had something in common because I've spent my whole childhood with a sense of not belonging, and I was sure that I was adopted. I felt there was no way these could be my birth parents.

I learned from a very young age to become self-reliant. My parents were so busy making ends meet and just surviving out here in Australia that I had to figure out how to do things for myself.

As a toddler, I wasn't very affectionate. At least that is what my parents have told me. That and the fact that I was a fussy eater. I was not a cuddly child, and I enjoyed playing on my own most of the time. If someone tried to play with my toys, I became annoyed at them. I didn't like being hugged or kissed too much, and I imagine that for two people who had spent their entire lives yearning for love, this must have been difficult for my parents.

Perhaps I was aloof and liked playing on my own so much because my parents were working so hard all the time and must have been exhausted when they were home. They were in a foreign country struggling to make ends meet in the beginning. They were learning a new language with no family or friends to support them. It took lots of courage for my parents to immigrate to Australia on their own, especially as I was born a few short years after their arrival just to spice things up a little bit.

My Mom worked the night shift in a factory. Dad worked long hours during the day as a bricklayer building houses. They worked these jobs so that one of them could always be with me as I was growing up. I had Mom during the day and Dad at night-time for a while.

We moved around a lot with my Dad's work. Just to give you an idea, we had moved thirteen times by the time I was six years old. If we couldn't live closer to Dad's work for whatever reason, there would be weekends when he would stay on site because it was too far for him to come back home.

This chapter is the shortest of all the chapters, as I only have memories of what happened before I was five years old, with little recollection of any thoughts. The only ideas I can recall were sheer and utter joy, wonder, and curiosity.

For example, I had a fascination with snails and the silver trails they left behind. Spending my mornings collecting as many as I could find in the garden, just to watch them slither away and leave these silver lines behind them. In my mind, they were magical.

Sofia, the first of my cousins, arrived in Australia shortly after my third birthday. She was also the firstborn child in her family and only six months older than I. We must have made an instant connection as we have been best friends our entire lives. It could be that we always found ourselves in the same boat: with parents in a foreign country who couldn't speak the language and spent most of their days working to provide us with everything we needed to live. At least now we had each other and our love for one another. When we were together, nothing else mattered.

A year later, my cousins Christopher and Maria arrived in Australia. Maria would be crucial to me throughout my childhood. She was four years older than I, and it always felt like she was our mother hen, watching over us and making sure that we were safe.

I always felt so loved when I was with her. She was what I associated with unconditional love. Her brother, Christopher, taught us just to have fun and be silly. He always knew how to make us laugh. Christopher was a year older than I, and he was the clown. As you can see, I was the youngest of the pack, at least for the time being.

My cousins coming to Australia was a critical moment in my life because no matter what I have been through, our love for each other has always remained constant. I knew they were always there for me, and I knew that they adored me as much as I adored them. I could always count on their love whenever I needed it, and I had an infinite amount of love to give to them if they ever needed it. It was a love I gave away happily, no strings attached. I never needed anything in return. It just made me happy to be a part of their lives and have them in my life.

Another memory I have is of my parents buying a puppy dog. His name was Floppy. He was a Jack Russell terrier. I think my parents brought him home so that I would have company. Memories seem to have such an impact at this early age. Before I turned five, a huge German shepherd attacked our little dog. *Jack Russells are very territorial and over-protective of their families, and I think they forget their size.*

My parents told me that he was at the vet's and would be home soon. They were hoping that I would forget about him, being so young, and eventually, stop asking about him. I guess they didn't know how to explain to a four-year-old that he had died. After weeks of me waiting at the window for Dad's arrival in the hope that I would see my dog again, my parents sat me down and told me that he wasn't coming back home.

To this day this memory haunts me. I have been taking our

dogs for walks for many years, but dogs off lead have attacked my dog who is nine years old. My dog has been attacked four times now. I know I have attracted these events with my thoughts about this old fear, but it is so deep in my subconscious mind that specific help will be required to overcome this issue.

Overcoming this fear is currently on my to-do list. It doesn't help that years later my parents brought home another dog of the same breed and he died in the same way. Not with the same German shepherd, though!

Moving along, I remember a trip to the hospital at the age of four to have my tonsils removed. I was so thrilled to be in the hospital because I could eat as much ice cream and jelly as I wanted. When I came out of the operation, my parents surprised me with a gorgeous doll that was half my height. She was the biggest princess I had ever seen. She was beautiful.

There was a much older girl in the bed next to mine. She would have been about ten years old. She asked if she could play with my doll when my parents had left, and as I wasn't feeling well enough to play with her myself, I didn't see the harm. When I woke up after many hours of sleep, she returned the doll to me. My doll was now broken. She didn't apologize for breaking it. Her parents didn't offer to replace her with a new one. She broke my toy before I even got to play with her and all I got from my Mom was that it was my fault because I should never have let that older girl play with it.

This incident would have upset my Mom immensely. This doll would have been very costly to my parents, and she was heartbroken that I didn't even get to play with her myself. Her reaction was her way of dealing with the anger of someone else breaking my doll. This event has taught me not to get attached to things.

This lesson would repeat itself over and over again in my life. It also taught me not to trust others with my belongings because they don't care. Today I have learned that how we treat our belongings and the possessions of others, says a lot about how we feel about ourselves.

Other memories I have of this time in my life are of my Dad teaching me how to brush my teeth. Bindies in the garden and bee stings because they were both so painful, how can you forget that? I also recall a creek that ran on the other side of the road.

I remember being under five when Mom and I would travel on the bus or a train, and staring at strangers. Mom was always telling me that it was rude and that I shouldn't stare, but I knew that if I kept looking at them, that eventually they would look at me. When they did finally make eye contact, I would smile, and they always smiled back. I never had a stranger that didn't smile back, and this made me feel connected to that person.

In reality, my Mom was trying to keep me safe as she thought the world was a dangerous place and that I was too trusting. She was worried that this would not be good in the future when I was older. The world being a hostile place was the one thing that was continually reinforced throughout my childhood. That the world is not a safe place and that you can't trust anyone except Mom and Dad.

Now I distinctly remember one morning, I had a play date with a friend the same age as me. Her name was Caroline. Outside in the garden, we found all these red berries on a bush and decided we were going to make medicine with them. We were crushing the little seeds into a bowl. The next minute, my friend was crying and screaming at the top of her lungs. "What on earth is wrong with her?" I thought. I rubbed my eyes and discovered exactly what was wrong with her. This stuff stings and burns and aaarrgghhhh. As four-year-olds do, we just kept rubbing our eyes hoping the pain would subside, but it just got worse. Eventually, our parents washed our eyes out with a lot of water and the pain slowly disappeared.

I was extremely curious about death. I'm not sure why. I also don't know if we are all born with this curiosity or if it was just me. I remember at the age of four being fascinated with death. One morning, my Mom walked into my room, and I was holding my breath pretending I was dead. Well, I can tell you when she started screaming and crying, I started breathing again. I wanted to know what it felt like to be dead. What does it mean to be dead? But I think, more importantly, the question was: What happens when you die?

Now age four was a pretty exciting time because I had been watching Sesame Street for years and they kept talking about this amazing place called school. At four I was allowed to start preschool, and I could not wait to get started. I had a love of learning, and as neither of my parents had a complete education, I had to figure things out on my own, at least until I could read by myself.

My first day of preschool was such a disappointment. All I remember doing that day was sticking cotton wool to a piece of paper to pretend they were clouds in the sky. But I wanted to know how the clouds form and why is the sky blue and where does the water come from when it rains... I had so many questions and sticking cotton wool to a piece of paper with glue was not quite what I had in mind when I said I wanted to learn about the world.

At preschool, I discovered another concept that I knew nothing about it. Most of the other children talked about having brothers and sisters. What are brothers and sisters? Why don't I have one? They sound like fun. Maria and Christopher hadn't arrived from Argentina yet. It was just Sofia and me at this point.

I should ask Mom and Dad if we can get one because

apparently, that's who you ask if you want one of those. I felt that it was imperative to have one too. Having a sister felt important in my life. Like it was something I needed to have. I didn't want to be the only one missing out on these amazing things called siblings.

So, several months after my fifth birthday my sister Anna was born. She was named after my Grandmother on my Mom's side of the family. My life as I knew it was over. My sister was getting all of my mom's attention, all of my mom's affection, all of my Mom. All of my Mom belonged to her now. I was devastated. In my eyes, I was dead to my Mom. Unwanted, unlovable, obsolete. This moment is where I developed a sense of invisibility.

In truth, now that I can see with clarity, my Mom was just giving my sister the same amount of care and attention that she had given me when I was born. I couldn't remember that my mother had done all of that for me five years before my sister's birth. As I was now Miss Independent because I am five years old, all I could see was that Mom no longer wanted me. I assumed that she preferred my sister.

So I became a Daddy's girl because I didn't want my Mom to know how much she had hurt me. I pretended that I was all right and happy and didn't care that I felt tossed aside like a toy that you no longer want to play with because you have a new one. Feeling so betrayed, I felt that you can't trust anyone because they will only take their love away. Just like my Mom had done. I was so angry with her. How dare she treat me like I am nothing? Like I don't matter. Like I am invisible! And the most difficult question of all that I asked myself for most of my life: "Why bring me into the world if she didn't want me?"

My Dad's love has never changed. It has always been my rock. Whenever things got rough, there was always this place I could go to where I felt safe and loved. It was my first introduction to unconditional love. He was my hero and more than anything I wanted to be just like him when I grew up. He loved me just as I was. I never had to earn his love or win his approval. He just loved me.

Why was I excluded from all of my sister's activities when she was a baby? My Mom said that she didn't have my sister so that she would be a burden to me. She didn't like it when other moms had several children, and the eldest had to care and tend for their younger siblings. I guess this is how she had grown up. My Mom practically raised her two sisters, as my great aunt had her hands full with her children. Mom believed that it was her duty to raise my sister and that I should be free to be a kid... to have fun, to be silly, to be carefree.

My cousins were all going through something similar in their lives because we never questioned our love for each other. We leaned on each other when we felt unwanted, and knew that we were all the same. Living similar experiences. Especially for my cousin Sofia. She was going to have a little sister born eight months after my sister Anna was born. Her name was Isabella. My cousin's mother was born in Italy. Hence, the beautiful Italian names.

Boy were we in the same boat. But we never talked about these things. My cousins and I lived in the moment, whenever we got together. Not a care in the world. We had as much fun as we could. Never stopping to think of anything. Our top priority was to be with each other.

My cousins had to watch over their younger siblings. It was their responsibility to make sure that Christopher and Isabella were safe. My aunts would punish Sofia and Maria for not watching over the younger ones properly. If Christopher or Isabella hurt themselves or got into trouble, they were held accountable. I didn't have to look after Anna. So, I guess, I was lucky in that regard.

For the most part, I acted like my sister wasn't even there. My Mom didn't include me in helping to feed her or change her or be a part of anything that had to do with Anna, so I assumed that she was a separate thing to me. After my sister's birth, I had so many thoughts about myself and the world.

Firstly, I believed that I was separate from everything else. Secondly, you can't rely on love, because it can be taken away from you. Thirdly, material things will only be confiscated from you, so there's no point getting attached to them.

In all honesty, my parents were giving me a sister because I asked for one and because they thought that when they passed away, I would have someone that is still family. They have told me this many times, so giving me a sister was an act of love. Love for me, that I may never be alone without family in my life.

Another memory I have at the age of five was taking a drive in our car with Dad. I was in the back seat with my cousin Sofia, and I was fiddling around with the door handle. In those days, wearing seat belts was not mandatory. I was staring at a church steeple at the time when Dad turned a corner quite sharply. The next thing I knew, the door flew open and I was tumbling outside on the ground. My Dad said he got the fright of his life.

I don't remember any pain from this incident. The main reason I remember that this event took place was that for many years throughout my childhood, my right cheek was bright red. I have many photographs before I started high school with this bright red cheek. It looked ever so funny to have one scarlet cheek while the other one was pale.

At five years of age, I was starting Kindergarten, and I couldn't wait because I was finally going to learn about everything in the world. At least, that is what I thought. I spent the first few months in a class called ESL (English as Second Language). I was learning words that were so easy to put together, just because my parents didn't know how to speak English well.

My parents had deliberately made a choice not to speak English at home so that my sister and I would know how to speak a second language. I knew how to speak English from watching television. Sesame Street, Playschool and other educational shows on television had already taught me how to spell small words and all about numbers. I was bored out of my brain. Would I ever learn real stuff about the world?

Finally, my teachers figured out that I could speak English and very well. So I began attending the mainstream class, and my love affair with learning has never stopped. I loved reading from a very young age so when I discovered the school had a library and we could borrow books for free, I was over the moon.

Soon after my sister's birth, my self-image took a blow from an innocent comment my mom made. I wish to include this memory because I want you to see how easy it is to misinterpret the words of adults and others when you are a child. Everything has to do with you and what you are or what you are not. She said that my Dad had always wanted to have a son and she was sad that she had only given him girls. How could he do boys things with me? Or even bond with me?

My Dad could have loved me more if I had been born a boy. That's how I interpreted this comment. We could have had a stronger connection because we'd have more in common. So I tried as much as possible when I was growing up not to be "girly."

I'd learn to fish and play football with my boy cousins because Dad loved soccer so much and that's what they did together. I'd even go camping with the guys. It made me feel that I was a disappointment to him because I was a girl and that he would miss out on so many beautiful moments just by being born the wrong sex. All of these activities were enjoyable to me, but I was doing all these things for him. To help him feel complete as a father.

Sometimes comments are made that seem perfectly harmless at the time, but it can have quite an impact on our minds as a child. How we interpret these words. What we make up about our place in the world. Where do we fit into the world with these ideas? For the most part, it makes us feel that we aren't right just the way we are. There must be something wrong with us.

If only I were smarter
If only I were taller
If only I were prettier
If only I were thinner
If only I were more athletic
If only I were a boy or a girl
Then they could love me more.

I write "love me more" deliberately as this indicates that you acknowledge they love you, but you are not good enough just as you are right now, to be adored entirely at this moment. You need to be something else to be **perfect.**

At this point, I would encourage you to please go back and look at the first five years of your life. Your thought processes are so different throughout this period than in any other time that you have experienced. Now is an excellent opportunity to sit quietly and think about this time in your life.

Write down all the events that you can remember.

Make sure that you write down what happened. Just the simple facts.

Write down your interpretation of each event.

I wanted to tell you my story so that you can see how your life can turn upside down with one simple misinterpretation. It wasn't even something that was done to me or said to me. It was what I made up about myself by what I observed. You may have had something said to you or done to you to make you feel unwanted or unloved.

Either way, one day you will understand that this was all for you, so that you may know who you are. You need to know that you are joy. Love, compassion, patience, wisdom, beautiful are *who you are*. You are *all* these things and so much more. You always have been. If you haven't endured tremendously difficult situations in your life, you cannot experience strength or courage. Without these tough moments in your life, how can you know how resilient you truly are?

If possible, ask the person who "hurt" you for more information. How they remember it. What were they going through at the time? If it is an adult, the memory will be very different for them. **Asking the other person for information is not about placing blame on that person.** It is about trying to understand what they were going through so that you can realize that it had nothing to do with you in the first place.

If you knew that you were a mistake, or were unplanned or unwanted, as a result of someone's actions or words, it is time to release those thoughts. Your parents may not have been able to love you or express their love to you in a way that you understood. Adults often close off their hearts, so they don't have to feel pain anymore. It is a natural instinct. We were never meant to live a life of feeling dreadful all the time. So we shut off. This is not to say that you cannot be loved and that you are not worthy of being loved. It means that *they could not love*.

The easiest way to know yourself to be love is to give love. You can look for other children and other adults that have been treated in this way. Show them love and kindness. Let them know that even if you can't get it from your parents, it doesn't mean that you have to live a whole life without it. Only **you** can connect with them on a deeper level. Only people who have been through the same experience as you, can fully understand how it feels.

It's up to you to **be** the change you wish to see in your life. **It has always been your choice**. It's funny because change starts with you. It cannot be any other way. Modifying the way you view the world, alters everything inside the universe. Because you have now chosen to look at the world in a different light, others react and respond to you differently.

My Dad spoke to his father many years after they had all left home and he asked him why he had given them such brutal beatings. Granddad replied that all of his children had come out responsible, upstanding citizens of society, because of this extreme punishment. Why change something that had worked for so many generations? He was the only son that approached my grandfather to ask him this question before he passed away.

The truth is that my Dad managed to turn it all around. Somehow, he understood that **love** is all there is. We have no other reason to be here but to be an expression of that love. Just because someone couldn't love you when you were a child, it doesn't mean that you cannot give love to others. You make a promise to yourself, that what has happened to you will never happen to another person.

My Dad waited to have his children so that he could give us all that love that he never received as a child, but wished with all his heart that he had. He never smacked us or yelled at us and yet we respected him. We valued his advice and his opinion. We always thought that what he had to say was important. We listened to him because he always made time to hear what we had to say. He was never too busy to sit down and talk to us.

What was that person going through at the time? Knowing

what they were going through may give you clarity as to how this event took place. If they were lashing out at you, it might be a good opportunity to make peace with the fact that they were in so much pain that they felt the urge to let that out on you. As a result, it seems like they are attacking you at the time, but the truth is they don't know another way to express these feelings about themselves.

What happened to you, was never about you. It was always about the other person and acknowledge yourself for how strong you are that you survived that situation and are still standing here today.

I like to think of the past in this way. When we search for gold, we need to go through a lot of dirt or sand to find that tiny little sparkle from that very precious metal. The past is the same. You need to sift through a lot of dirt and thoughts that are covered with mud and grime to get to that moment of clarity. There is gold in every moment that you have experienced. You just need to make an effort to sift through all the muck to get to it. Keep digging through the dirt and the gold will eventually reveal itself to you.

Finally, I believe that we need to forget who we are to know who we truly are. Forgetting is a necessary process in life. How can you know that you are connected if you have never seen yourself as separate from everything? It is essential that we experience the opposite. How can we know light without dark and hot without cold? Therefore, we must know how it feels to live without love, to know what it is.

Furthermore, how can we know the truth about ourselves, without the lies we have been telling ourselves our whole lives? We cannot know ourselves to be at peace if we have not experienced the raging war within our mind. One cannot exist without the other. How can you know you are at peace if peace is all you have ever experienced? Due to cruel people, we can experience kindness because their actions create opportunities for others to express their love and compassion.

The most important thing to get out of this activity is the following:

1. What did you decide about the world?

2. How do you view others because of the decisions you made at this point in your life?

3. Who do you think you are?

4. What beliefs have you created about yourself?

5. Write down every memory you can remember about this time in your life. **It is the most significant time**. The first five years of our lives are where we are more susceptible to creating misinterpretations about ourselves and others.

Chapter 2

COLLECTING EVIDENCE

Mom yelled and spanked me quite often after my sister was born. This made me feel even more resentment towards my sister because as Anna became older, I would get into more trouble with Mom. The truth is, I never understood why I was punished. I just remember thinking, what have I done now?

Having more than one child is very challenging as they are always fighting and well, just being siblings. To the parent, it can be quite stressful though when they have to put up with the crying and the screaming that goes on. Also, in comparison with the punishment, my parents received as children, being smacked wasn't a big deal, when you come to think of it.

The only thing I learned from the yelling and the spanking was to fear my mother. I worked hard to be a "good" girl because I knew that being a "bad" girl, meant being punished. But I didn't know what it was to be a "good" girl. There were so many rules and the only rule I understood, was that you weren't allowed to make mistakes. If you accidentally spilled milk while pouring it or if you broke something accidentally, that was it. You were a "bad" girl. You were in big trouble.

So many good moments are canceled out with the smacking because we focus on the negative. It makes us feel that there is something wrong with us that we need to fix. As adults, we forget that children don't think the same as us. Their thoughts are not as complicated. They are very simple, and as adults, we have forgotten how to process ideas in this way.

We don't understand that often, children are just exploring their world. They drop things on the floor to study the effect of it falling. They are learning about cause and effect. When they make a mess with their food, they think they have created a masterpiece.

Trying to avoid punishment taught me to blame others. I didn't want to take responsibility for doing something because I knew I would get smacked for it. So I would lie and try to cover it up, rather than let Mom know that I did something that would make her cranky. But now I felt conflicted because the church was against lies. Telling the truth meant getting into trouble with Mom, while not telling the truth meant that God would be cross with me. Avoiding chastisement was a game I could never win because even if I lied to my mother, God knew the truth, and He would be there to punish me in the end. Punishment, it seemed, was unavoidable. The only way was to be perfect all the time, and that was hard work. It was exhausting.

When I turned six, my parents finally decided to settle down and buy their first house. Settling down in our first home signified that we no longer had to move around. They bought a three bedroom fibro home one hour's distance away from Adelaide. We had one small bathroom and one tiny kitchen with a dining area. My Dad would spend many years renovating this house. Firstly, they extended to make room for a larger kitchen. Then Dad added a rumpus room and a second bathroom. Some of my uncles helped Dad cover the outside of the house with brick. It was gorgeous.

Living in a beautiful house would be a moment of awakening for me because like so many other people, I have spent many years as an adult, believing that if I had a magnificent house, I would be happy. I remember that it was incredible for a few years, but it was not enough to be completely contented and not have any more problems. We focus on all these external things because we don't want to address what is going on inside. They merely serve as distractions.

When I turned seven, the last of my cousins would arrive, Rita, along with my Grandmother. The cousins I had here in Australia, were all from my Dad's side of the family. We now had three of my Dad's brothers living here with my Dad's mom and us. I only talk of my cousins and not my aunts or uncles because as children we were treated as separate from the adults.

The adults would have their table to eat at, and we would eat at the little kid's table. They had their own "adults' talk," and we were told to go be kids and play together outside. So I don't remember having conversations with my aunts and uncles growing up here in Australia.

I recall my Grandmother being so tall as she was the same height as my dad, and he was six feet tall. I always felt that she was looking down on me and that was quite intimidating. This woman was all about discipline and respecting your elders. She was stern and not very warm at all, so it made it difficult to get close to her.

By grade three, I was excellent at school. I loved reading and learning and pretty much everything about school. Even sports day was fantastic, as I enjoyed running and discovering what my body could do. Reading and learning were my obsessions at this age which didn't leave much time for making friends. The only issue I had was that I would not ask a question if I didn't understand something. I always assumed that what I was going to ask was something stupid. So I always took it on board to have to teach myself outside of class.

The only thing I didn't enjoy about school was doing art or craft. I found this pointless. What's the point of drawing or painting or sewing? It was all so messy. Coloring in was okay, but even then, I wasn't learning anything new.

I didn't like doing group projects either. Having to share my work with others that would not be able to keep up with my standards was not something I enjoyed. Not trusting that they would do it the way I thought we needed to do it. In truth, I had become quite a control freak. Having said that, I did enjoy playing team sports, because I wasn't attached to the outcome of these games. I just enjoyed the physical experience. Winning was not a concept that mattered to me.

I was fortunate enough that my parents bought me the World Encyclopaedia. Volumes and volumes of knowledge. I would spend many countless hours reading these books. Not only that, but we discovered the local library across from where we shopped every week for groceries. It was way bigger than the library at my school. So every week we borrowed books from this library and returned them the following week when we went to do our weekly shopping. I was in heaven.

Up to this point in my life, I think it's safe to say that I was elated. I would wake up each morning excited to see what the day had in store for me. Going to bed every night delighted about the wonderful day I had experienced. Fantasizing about what the following day would bring. Would it be as good as this day? Would I experience something new? What new things could I learn the next day? I had not a care in the world. My job was to experience each new day as it came. Life was good.

My relationship with my sister was straightforward. As long as she stayed out of my way, I was content. Anna had no idea how to keep herself entertained. She always needed someone else to play with her or be with her. Sometimes, I played with her, but I wasn't interested in anything that didn't involve reading or learning, and she was too young to play sports the way I wanted to. So I felt like spending time with her was a waste of my day.

In retrospect, Anna was one step ahead of me. I had closed myself off from the world. She knew that relationships were all that mattered. My sister didn't care for learning or reading. She just wanted to interact with my parents and me.

I didn't feel connected to my younger sister, and that could have been because I wasn't included in any of her activities when she was a baby. I couldn't feed her or change her nappies or even hold her. It felt very different to when I was with my cousins.

I spent all day at school and then when I got home, it was my special time to be with my Dad. Sometimes, we played games with my neighbors in the front yard. Most Saturdays we spent with our cousins and my sister had Isabella that was just a few months younger than her. They played well together, and I could enjoy time with my older relatives. I spent one season learning how to play chess with Maria, my eldest cousin. I loved that summer.

Doing handstands, learning to do cartwheels together. Rolling down hills at the beach, playing ping pong. Playing chasing at the park and riding bikes together. Being with our cousins was about having as much fun as possible and enjoying our time together. So I know what it is to live in the moment because when I was with them, nothing else existed. Before I was nine, we had two new additions to the group. Christopher and Maria had two cousins from their Mom's side of the family: Sonia and Paul. They became part of our family. It was like they were our real blood relatives as well.

There was one event at this time in my life that taught me a lot about myself. My cousin Christopher thought it was funny to push me and watch me fall, especially as more often than not, I would graze my knees or hands and I would cry. This pushing had been going on for quite a few months now. He was just learning the brilliant concept of cause and effect.

As I was the youngest in the group, I was the easiest to pick on. Christopher enjoyed producing such an interesting outcome each time. My Mom witnessed this over the course of many months and one day she said to me before they would all be arriving at our house: "Hollie, today when Christopher pushes you down, I want you to get back up and push him back as hard as you can."

This conduct went against everything my Mom had taught me because we were not allowed to hurt each other. I was not permitted to lay a finger on my sister, let alone my cousins. It also went against what we learned in church about turning the other cheek and all that. I guess there are only a certain amount of times you can turn your cheek before enough is enough and you need to find a solution to the problem. Still, I had no choice; this was my Mom telling me to do this. There was no way I wasn't going to obey her request. There must be a good reason that Mom would ask me to do this.

Looking back it taught me two valuable lessons: firstly, that I did not need to be afraid of bullies and secondly, that I could take care of myself. Chris cried like a baby, because he just wasn't expecting my reaction, and because it's not nice getting back what you've been dishing out for months. Suddenly it wasn't so amusing because it had happened to him. But he never pushed me again.

Now, I am not condoning the action of retaliating towards someone who is bullying you. I don't believe that it is the answer. The truth is that bullies thrive on your reaction to their actions. A bully does not have much to look forward to, once you remove the reaction out of the equation. Pushing back worked for me at that time in my life, and I am grateful for that wisdom.

23

Then the unimaginable happened. My third-grade teacher told my Mom that I was smart and that I had come fourth in my class for that year. I didn't come first because I never handed in any homework. After school was my special time to be with my Dad. I hadn't seen him all day, and I wasn't going to waste time doing silly homework when I could be with him. My mother decided that it was a waste of a beautiful mind and a shame not to use it to its full potential. She wanted me to go to University and have all the opportunities my parents never had in their childhood.

So I was sent to Catholic School. This school is where I would get a superior education and learn about discipline. We even learned Latin at this school. Here is where I would discover who God truly was. But this made me feel that it was wrong to love my Dad. It forced me to feel guilty about wanting to be with him. Dad was the most beautiful human being I knew. I felt that I wasn't worthy of being with him and that this was the reason they punished me. In truth, I had always been afraid of him withdrawing his affection too. I mean, if it was so easy to lose my Mom, why wouldn't it be just as easy for him to take his love away?

My Mom was a devout Catholic. We had been going to church on Sundays for many years. So the concept of God was not new to me. The difference was that at Catholic School I was taught to fear God and his wrath. God was an all-powerful being with a long flowing beard that sits in the sky. He watches us in every moment, all of us because He has the power to be in all places simultaneously. God was always judging us because He had to decide whether we were good enough to come and live with Him when we die.

We were separate from this Supreme Being. He had a thing for suffering. I mean, look at all the stories of the saints. The more they suffered, the more worthy they were of His love. We spent most of the time at Mass kneeling on wooden boards that made your knees ache by the end of the Sermon. It was just a reminder that the more pain you felt, the more you pleased God. He was such an angry guy according to the Old Testament. He was always punishing people for not listening. They just couldn't follow simple instructions:

I forbid you to eat the apples from that tree!
You will turn into salt if you look back!
I don't want you to idolize idols!

The list goes on. I guess I might have felt frustrated too. I felt sorry for God. He made us in His own image, and we were such a disappointment. We couldn't even love His son Jesus. We had to crucify him. God could see all things at all times, just like Santa. Except Santa was a jolly fellow. It didn't matter if you were naughty. He just didn't leave you any presents. It wasn't the end of the world. But God's job was to watch us, not in a protective fatherly way, but more like this scornful judge in a courtroom up in the sky. He was judge, jury, and prosecutor, deciding our fate after death. In truth, God was not the Being I feared.

At Catholic School, they introduced me to the Devil. Apparently, it was so easy to go to Hell. I mean this guy meant business. The Devil was always looking for new recruits even though Hell was already overcrowded with lost souls. At this school they made it sound like getting into Heaven was impossible and going to Hell was inevitable for most of us. From this point on I was always afraid. No matter what I did, it never seemed good enough to get me into Heaven. The Devil had the same powers as God. He could see all and be in all places at the same time.

Then we learned that pets don't go to Heaven. We also learned that you have to be baptized if you want to enter

Heaven. My Dad was an atheist. He didn't believe in God. So now I felt conflicted. If my Dad couldn't get into this exclusive club, then I didn't want to go either. But going to Hell sounded so unappealing when you had this beautiful Heaven to go to instead. It didn't seem fair that my Dad had to go to Hell. He was the kindest most loving person I had ever known. Nobody deserved to go to Heaven more than my Dad.

At school, prayers were never about giving thanks or being grateful for anything. Prayers were when you asked God for the things you wanted the most. So the majority of my prayers were about please don't let me go to Hell and is there anything you can do to help my Dad not go to Hell too, please? I also spent most of my prayers saying I was sorry for this and sorry for that because I didn't want God to be angry with me for doing anything wrong.

It was around this time that my Dad shared his views on God and death. According to my Dad when you die you get buried in a box in the ground, and the worms eat you. That was it. There is nothing else. The end. My Mom overheard this conversation and told my Dad not to say that to me, that it wasn't true because she believed in God and all the angels.

Mom felt when her parents died, that the Virgin Mary came to visit her to console her. Deep down, I presumed what my Mom said was true, because I knew somewhere inside me, that spirit exists and that even though our physical body may be thrown into a wooden box and fed to the worms when we die, our spirit lives on. We are never ending.

My Dad couldn't understand how there could be a God. How can He exist when children are starving in the world? Why does He allow so much suffering to take place on earth? How can God just sit idly by and not "fix" everything so that we can all be at peace and have everything we need to live? Why do some have everything, while others have nothing?

I can understand him being cynical as he was one of those children that went hungry when he was little. He was one of those children in the world that had one pair of shoes that had to last him three years. He barely had clothes to keep him warm in winter. I can imagine him being an infant suffering, wondering, God, if you do exist, where are you? How can you let me suffer? A child that has done nothing wrong and is pure and innocent.

So this is what I grew up with: two very opposing views. My Dad was convinced that God could not exist because of the state of the world. God could not just watch and do nothing. Therefore, there is no God. I believed my Mom. I accepted that a spirit came to comfort her because she was in so much grief at her loss when her parents passed away. The spirit came to her in a form that she could readily recognize and accept. This vision came to tell her that she was not alone, that someone was watching over her at all times, and that she would be okay.

At Catholic school, I would make my first real friend, or so I thought. Her name was Michelle. She lived in the street behind mine. We spent every recess and every lunch time together, just the two of us. I felt so lucky to have her. I could stop thinking about all the things we learned about God and the Devil.

Being my best friend, I had to invite her to my birthday party. I waited all afternoon looking out our front window, but she never came. Not only that but when we got back to school, she wouldn't even talk to me. She had made friends with another girl and would completely ignore me when I tried to talk to her. I felt so alone now that I had no company. How was I supposed to deal with all the thoughts of the Devil by myself? These thoughts plagued my mind without Michelle. I had become invisible once again.

In truth, I was just gathering proof of how unsafe it is to love someone because they can easily replace you with someone else. Just like my Mom had done all those years before.

At about this time, my Mom had made friends with a lady that had just arrived from Argentina. We called her Aunt Lucy even though she wasn't a blood relative of ours. She was obsessed with my sister. Great! More people to make me feel invisible and unwanted. She was so obvious though that it made me feel faulty. Like I had come damaged from the factory, and would never work properly.

It didn't help that my Grandmother passed away that same year. Now, my Grandmother had come to Australia just two years before she died. She was the mother of all our dads. My cousins were my cousins because our dads were all brothers. There were several reasons I didn't like her.

The first one was that she used to spend one week at each son's house. When it was her turn to visit our home, all she did was compare what her other sons were doing with their children and how my Mom was doing it all wrong. She was always giving my Mom grief about how lenient she was with my sister. That Mom didn't discipline her and that Anna did whatever she wanted. All these issues almost caused my Mom to have a nervous breakdown. I remember Mom crying, talking to Dad about him always taking sides with his mother and never taking Mom's side. Not once. She put a lot of pressure on my parents.

The second reason was that my parents had given my sister and me a huge teddy bear each. I wasn't more than nine years old, but I used to dry hump my bear on my bed. I rubbed my private bits on him, and after a few minutes, it gave me great pleasure. Nobody had taught me to do this. It was purely instinctual. I was just exploring and discovering my body and what it could do. I was enjoying my sexuality. My Grandmother walked in on me one day, and after that, my parents took the bears away. I felt like I had done something wrong and felt ashamed, but didn't know why.

Again, I just loved discovering what my body could do. How high could I jump? How fast could I run? What happens when I play down there with my teddy bear? It tickles and tingles and feels funny. But it never felt wrong. What felt bad was how the adults around me reacted to it.

Like what you learned in Catholic school wasn't bad enough. How your body is sinful, that it is dirty and something shameful. The Church always talked about the body like it was something unclean and disgusting and sex was something evil. How could we feel good about looking at ourselves in the mirror, when we learned that the body is pretty much the filthiest thing on the planet? Sex was the work of the Devil. It's not like you have to have sex to procreate or anything like that.

After having many sessions with a therapist trying to work through my issues in my adult life, I discovered that this behavior is natural. It is perfectly normal for children to explore their private parts and their sexuality. There was absolutely nothing wrong with what I had done.

The third reason was that I had to share my room with my Grandmother and she used to snore very loudly. Every night, I would lie down and hear her pray. It sounded like a mumble from my bed, but I knew that's what she was doing. One night she went to bed, and I couldn't hear her praying, and she wasn't snoring. I was worried. What if she had died right next to me? I got up very slowly and carefully because if she was asleep, I didn't want to wake her up. I was about to put my head on her chest to see if I could hear her breathing when she jumped up and told me to go back to my bed in a very stern voice. She gave me the fright of my life.

My Grandmother didn't interact much with any of us except to discipline us for doing something wrong. She was not very

Insufficient.

affectionate or kind. So most of us, as in her grandchildren, did not feel any great loss when she passed. But now something else stirred in my brain. I couldn't go to the funeral. It was my only chance to see a dead body. Maybe I could understand death a little better.

After these two events, losing my friend and losing my Grandmother, I would go to sleep crying and I would wake up crying every morning. A new fear had grabbed hold of me. When people die, they don't come back. What if Mom and Dad die? Who will take care of us? I was afraid to go to school because there I was continually reminded that the Devil was waiting to take my soul. I cried if I had to enter a church because I felt that the body is something sinful and vile. It is impure and repugnant. How could I stand in God's house when I was so unworthy of being in His presence? Unfortunately, He was the only person where I could not be invisible. He saw all things at all times, remember?

After months and months of crying, I started having problems with my teeth. I had to go to the dentist for my first filling. My first needle injected into my gums. As a young child, this was absolutely terrifying. My Dad took me to the dentist. As we were sitting in the waiting room, he told me that if I cried or screamed, he would walk out of the dentist's room and leave me in there all alone with him. I crushed his hand with my grip but didn't even whimper because I didn't want to embarrass him. Nor did I want to be left alone with a complete stranger.

My Dad said he was so proud of me and that I was such a tough little girl. What this taught me, was that to be strong was not to show emotions. Hiding my feelings was something I would learn to master. It also meant that many people would find me indifferent and aloof. I was becoming skillful at hiding my feelings. I never cried when I watched sad movies. Mom taught us that feeling angry or sad was wrong. We had no reason to feel anything but happy. Dad taught me not to react to painful situations.

Eventually, after many months of misery, my parents pulled me out of Catholic School and sent me back to the public school I had attended previously. For the next two years, I became an overachiever. I was top of my class and top of my year. The teachers were so impressed with me that they chose me as School Captain in sixth grade. But we'll talk about that later as we are not quite there yet.

In truth, I wasn't interested in any of that. I just didn't want to go back to that horrible Catholic School. If all I needed to do was study hard to keep Mom happy, then that's what I did. I could do that. Learning came naturally to me, and sitting tests was easy because I knew exactly how to prepare for them to blitz them.

I tried making friends in primary school, but the girls were into gossip, and I couldn't understand the point of this. My cousins and I never talked about anyone else. We just played and had fun and loved each other. So somewhere deep down I knew that I needed to avoid this behavior. What do you gain by saying negative things about others while they are not in front of you? You don't even give them the chance to defend themselves.

How did this help the person that was criticized and more importantly how did this make the gossipers better people? Besides, it went against what we had learned in Church. What gives you the right to judge a person for the splinter in their eye when you have a whole log in your eye? The whole point was to be a good person and help others and be kind.

So I spent most of my spare time in the library devouring book after book. It was my escape from the real world. I spent the rest of primary school trying to find answers. As much as they taught us that getting into heaven was impossible, there was a part of me that believed that I might still have a chance. After all, I had never stolen anything from anyone. I had never killed anyone, and I had never committed adultery. At least, not yet anyway. That's got to count for something, right?

At the age of ten, my love affair with music began. One that would last me my entire life. My parents sat me down one day and asked me if I would like to learn a musical instrument or something to do with music. The first thing I blurted out was "I want to learn piano!" My parents didn't know what to say. All of my dad's side of the family played the guitar and sang, and all of my mom's side were singers.

So where did I get the idea that I wanted to learn piano? I blame it on a record my parents used to play when I was quite young. It was Liberace playing Tchaikovsky's Piano Concerto Number 1 on the piano, along with his beautiful Waltz of the Flowers.

My parents couldn't afford to buy me a piano straight away, so we made an arrangement with the school. They gave me permission to go in every morning at 8 o'clock with the janitor to practice on the school piano. I did this for two years in a row and the only time I missed my practice was when I was in the hospital (but that was when I turned eleven, so you'll hear about that in the next chapter).

Now I have to tell you that from the first moment I produced a sound on that instrument, words cannot describe the sheer pleasure I felt from translating the black and white scribble on a page into something fantastic to hear. The first piano teacher I took lessons from, had me on two bars of music for almost eight weeks. My fingers had to be curved correctly. The expression of the six notes on the page had to be perfect. The timing, the dynamics, the rhythm - perfect. I had been working on six music notes for eight lessons. I was bored out of my mind! Surely, there had to be more to music than this?

For those who don't have any musical knowledge, this is the equivalent of being allowed to read a book except you are only reading the first six words of the story, and you have to read those six words correctly. The tone of your voice, the enunciation of each letter, how slowly you read it, etc. Not even six sentences. No, just six words for eight weeks! Now, do you understand my frustration?

My next piano teacher was great, but he was forty minutes away, so he didn't last long either. Three teachers later, we found a very experienced piano teacher. (Just a nice way of saying pretty old). She was great in the sense that she gave me loads of music to play. I had four books each lesson plus my theory book. I learned a great deal from her about how *not* to teach piano. Rule number one: do not tell your student who is only ten years old that they are too old to be a concert pianist.

This comment crushed my spirit, but in time I learned something invaluable. How odd is it, that to one student that comment would stop them from achieving their dream, while to another student this would be the catalyst that propels them forward to complete that goal, just to prove her wrong? Everyone and everything is on our path to thrust us into knowing who we are. Knowing what we are capable of achieving and what we can do if we just believe in ourselves. **Everything is a gift for you.**

I remember that I loved playing the piano just for me. Spending hours playing just for the joy of producing those amazing sounds on this remarkable instrument. Playing for others never really interested me. I always felt judged for any mistakes made. These errors were a reflection of me not practicing enough or not being good enough.

When I played for myself, I didn't care about how perfect it was; I just cared about the sound and how beautiful it was to my ears. Not only that, but I had two hands working in perfect harmony to create this magnificent music. My left hand would learn to be equal to my right, and that in itself was pretty cool. Just watching the fingers do their work and learn and respond to new skills year after year.

I naturally heard variations in my mind at this young age. I would be learning a piece, and I could hear all sorts of wonderful different ways to arrange it. The only problem was that in class we had to play the notes that were on the page. Apparently, what I was doing was not music, just as jazz was not music. The right kind of music to learn on the piano when I was young, was classical music and that is such a shame. Jazz music has such complex rhythms. It is fascinating.

So I had to learn this in my spare time. Mom bought me a book of ragtime pieces composed by Scott Joplin. I loved that book. Going shopping with mom was a beautiful memory in itself. Mom spent a whole morning in the City with me at the largest music shop she could find, so that I could buy some piano books that I wanted to learn for myself. It was full of instruments and rows upon rows of music books. It was a magical day for me.

The best part about learning music is that you watch yourself achieve things that you thought were impossible. Overcoming these obstacles is such a confidence booster. You start off looking at a piece thinking there is no way I can do that, and with patience, I mean, a lot of patience, you whittle away at it until you have mastered this new skill. It gives you such great confidence in yourself that you can achieve anything.

The good news about learning music was that I didn't have to think about God anymore. I decided not to waste my time thinking about Him because chances were that I'd never end up being with Him anyway. I could never be good enough, and there was nothing I could do about that. So I just focused on the pieces of music I was learning and was always looking forward to what I would be playing next.

Another wonderful memory I have of this time in my life. I was learning to play tennis on Saturday mornings. Most Sundays my Dad and I would get up early, and we would go to local high schools to practice. These high schools had tennis courts, and in those days we were allowed to play on these. The schools didn't have fences around them, nor did they have signs saying you can't play on these grounds.

Sometimes we played from six in the morning till almost midday. I love these memories because at least Dad and I had something we enjoyed together, just the two of us. It made me feel special that he made time to be with me. We also had a ping pong table at home that we played on. The table tennis game was for everyone. Even the cousins played with us here. It was lots of fun.

What I do remember about my mom was that she attended all my events. If I had to play at a piano concert, she was always there to watch me. She didn't miss anything that was important to me. She even sat to watch me play tennis every Saturday morning with my coach.

Now here's a funny memory for you. Talk about being innocent. Growing up, we all had different colored towels, so we each knew which one belonged to us. When I was ten years old, I remember taking a shower one day and when I had finished, my towel wasn't there. Mom must have put it in the wash and forgot to put out a new one for me. So I decided to pick up the yellow towel that was sitting there. After I had got dressed, I was sitting in my bedroom, and the thought hit me that I had used my dad's towel to dry.

I couldn't stop crying. My Mom walked in on me and found me distraught. I told her that I was pregnant. I felt mortified. She looked confused and asked me to please explain why I thought that. I told her that I had dried my body with dad's towel and that now I was going to have a baby. She laughed, of course, and assured me that I couldn't possibly be pregnant. I believed her, and that was that. End of discussion.

Growing up, I never wanted to be older or be like anyone else, because I was happy just being me and experiencing my life. Even though I was the youngest, I felt equal to my cousins. I could play with them at their level and didn't feel disadvantaged by the age gap. Maria and I learned to play chess when I was ten years old, and we both enjoyed learning this new game together. If I had to choose, the only person I wanted to be like, was my Dad, because, in my eyes, he was the closest you could get to being perfect.

My Mom started off with a simple smack on the bottom when I was little. Towards the end, she had to hit me with a wooden spoon when I got older because the hand on the bottom was no longer effective. The other thing that I realized was that one smack would erase a hundred happy moments because you focus on the fact that you did something "bad" and forgot all the positive things.

Recently talking to my cousin Sofia, we were discussing our moms and their smacking and yelling. Unfortunately, for a long time, that's all I could remember about my Mom. Sofia felt the same. We couldn't recall having any tender moments with them.

Most of the time you are just being a kid and exploring the world around you. I mean, who decides how many times you can spill milk before you can pour it correctly? Children need to make mistakes to learn. We all do. It's just that we are instructed from such a young age that mistakes are bad and we need to avoid them like the plague. So, we become afraid of learning because this means that you have to get it wrong many times before you get it right. Getting it wrong is how it works.

There are no instructions on how many times you need to err before it works. For some people maybe five times is enough. Others may require twenty times to learn how to do something, while others may never find out how to do it, no matter how much they try. But that's okay. That's life! Everything you learn is for you. For your personal growth.

Use this part of your workbook to recall any memories you have between five and ten years old.

Make notes of your thoughts and experiences at the time.

- What did someone say to you?

- How did you interpret these words?

- What did someone do to you?

- How did you translate these actions?

Look very carefully to see how many of these are of you collecting evidence about who you decided you were before you were five. For example, if you decided you were unwanted and cast aside, how many of these new memories reinforced this belief about yourself.

Once we decide something about ourselves, we go out into the world looking for evidence. We are regularly trying to confirm that our suspicions are right. As a result, more and more opportunities present themselves for us to prove our theories to be correct.

How many new beliefs have you gathered along the way about yourself and the world at this early age?

Chapter 3

WHAT ARE YOUR STRENGTHS?

Towards the end of primary school, I started having issues with my health. Before my 11th birthday, I was in and out of doctors due to pain in my groin. They thought I was getting my first period (whatever that was). My parents had never talked to me about menstruation or anything to do with sex. In my home, sex, death, and money were subjects that you did not discuss with children when we were growing up.

It turns out that I had appendicitis. I ended up in the hospital one month after I turned eleven. At the time I couldn't be more thrilled as that would mean that I had to miss out on the swimming carnival at school. It was one of the few activities I did not enjoy at school. Not knowing how to swim was something that I would soon regret, though.

I remember crying that first night my parents had to leave me there and telling my Mom that I would be good and that I would help more with the housework, but please don't leave me here all alone. After they had left, I realized that being alone in the hospital wasn't so bad after all. I was in a ward with many other children and the boy in the bed next to me had also had his appendix removed. He had been there for four days, and he was leaving the next day.

The nurses said that for him to leave, he had to be able to cough so that they could let him go. They needed to make sure the stitches wouldn't pop. Coughing was extremely painful for him, but I found this so funny that I couldn't stop laughing and that in itself was excruciating. So by the end of it, we were both in tears. Mine were tears of laughter, and he was crying tears of pain because he wanted to go home the next day.

I spent the rest of this year with sinus problems. Again I was in and out of doctors trying to find relief from the pain in my sinuses and the constant stuffiness in my nose. I was finding it difficult to breathe properly. The headaches were becoming less and less bearable, and nothing seemed to be working.

We have finally reached the year I became School Captain. This year was pretty exciting for me at school. I remember making lots of speeches at assembly. I was chosen because I had been top of my class and top of my year for the past year and because I was good at sports too. Something odd happened to me in this year though that I found difficult to understand. It gave me doubts about justice and the right thing to do.

One day we were having a maths test as was customary at the end of each week to make sure that we understood what the teacher taught us in that week. We used to have one for spelling as well. When the test was over, we would swap our books with the row behind us. The teacher would then give us the answers so that we could mark each other's work. The girl sitting next to me would rub out any mistakes for the book she was marking. Then she would write in the correct answer for her friend, Jane. This girl Jane lived right next door to me. She was my neighbor.

Changing the answers was cheating! I told my teacher at the end of the test what I had witnessed, and she said that I was jealous of Jane. At the end of the previous year, she had also been at the top of her class. (We used to have two different classes for each grade). This was the first year that I was in the same class as Jane.

I did not understand her response. Cheating is cheating! To me this was unacceptable. How is it fair that she was top of her class when she had someone change her answers, so she got a perfect score every time?

Many years later I discovered that Jane's mother had complained when they made me School Captain, and she was saying that it was not fair because I had missed a year of school there and that her daughter had been there the whole time. I did not know this, but I assume now, that my teacher thought there was a rivalry between us.

As far as I knew, she had been my neighbor for five years, and we were now in the same class for grade six. We had spent countless summers playing in our front yards with her twin brother. She had come to several of my birthdays over the years, and I had been to hers as well. That was it. I didn't even know she came first in her class the year before. I didn't care about any of that.

But again, I lost faith in adults. I had the highest respect for my teacher when the year had started, and with this incident, I learned that adults aren't always just. Adults aren't always fair. Adults sometimes make no sense at all. How could I be jealous of someone that was no competition to me? I didn't see her as a threat at all.

I had to get good grades for my Mom, not for anyone else. It was never about anyone else. Other children did not exist when it came to schoolwork. It was never about being better than anyone else. I found maths easy to understand and had no problem remembering how to spell words or learning in general. Maths was my passion because, in school, maths meant just one possible answer to the question.

English was hard work for me. When we had comprehension, there could be various possible answers, and I didn't like the uncertainty of the outcome. Not knowing if my interpretation was the correct one. I just knew that I was good at schoolwork. It came naturally to me. I never doubted in my abilities when it came to studying and tests.

But once again, I was let down by an adult. Once again, I couldn't trust. This incident seemed unfair at the time. It felt like my teacher was calling me a liar and telling me that I had made the whole thing up. It's difficult to know where to turn to when you can't count on those you love and respect. I became withdrawn again, insular. That would teach me to never trust an adult again as a child.

Around this time I started having vision problems. My eyesight was getting blurry, so I needed to start wearing glasses. They weren't very common when I was young, but I was never aware of what others said about me. Nobody picked on me for looking different. Then again, I never listened to what other children said as in my mind they could not teach me anything new. Only books and teachers had knowledge and could help me learn about the world. I lived in my own little bubble and looking back now; this was such a blessing to me.

Towards the end of grade six, my parents decided to take a holiday to Argentina to visit all our relatives there. We had been writing to our aunts and uncles for years but had never met them. These few months were very exciting to me. Visiting Argentina was magical because, for the first time in my childhood, my Aunt Rita and Uncle Tony would interact with my sister and me.

This equal treatment was new to me. My Mom's sisters were interested in talking to us and finding out who we were. Aunt Rita and Aunt Rebecca, to this day, are my favorite aunts. They were the first of my family to treat me like I mattered and what I had to say was meaningful. I wasn't invisible to them. They treated Anna the same way, so I didn't feel that there was any favoritism.

We learned numerous card games throughout these summer months, and we played together. Sometimes we would play with the cousins, and sometimes my aunt and uncle would play with us too. It was the first time I didn't feel separate. We all ate at the same table. It was wonderful. For the first time in my life, I felt seen and heard and cherished. It was a vacation that I have treasured my entire life.

Many things happened during these few months away from home. I celebrated my 12th birthday in Argentina and got my first period a week later. At the time I thought I was dying. Blood was coming out of the spot where I usually pee. It was evident to me that one of my organs had exploded overnight and that's why there was blood. That also explained the cramping in my tummy. I was terrified. I was too scared to come out of the bathroom. Tears started streaming down my cheeks. I was only twelve years old. I was too young to be dying. Did something go wrong with my operation when they took out my appendix?

Sex and money were two topics that Mom and Dad never discussed in front of us. They were not appropriate for children. My parents sat me down and explained that this was healthy and natural. Not only that, but this was a monthly arrangement. Imagine my surprise, when I discovered that not only was I not dying, but that I was going to have these "periods" for the next forty years or so. I couldn't believe it. Really? Please tell me that this is a cruel joke, and one of my organs did in fact explode, and I am indeed dying.

At the time I felt like, what else am I not aware of that is going to happen to me? Was it going to be worse than this? I felt like there was so much out there that I didn't know. How could my parents let this happen to me and not warn me?

This time spent in Argentina would teach me many things,

but the most important one would be in the water. My Aunt Rebecca had a beach house. We had been to this beach several times throughout the week while we were staying there. The water was very shallow. We could walk towards an embankment that was about fifty meters away from the shore. The water never got more than waist high on me, and once we got to the embankment, it would be ankle high again.

We had been playing at this beach for about five days now. My thoughts throughout the week had been about a family that lived across from my Aunt's house. They obviously had money. They had a swimming pool, fancy clothes, and fancy cars and even played on a ping pong table. I so wanted to be spending the summer with them. Learning from them and understanding what they did that was different to my folks. Why were they allowed to have all this cool stuff while my family was always scraping by to make ends meet? They didn't seem corrupt or evil. I felt that something I had learned about money was not true.

On the second last day of our trip at this beach, we jumped into the water as we had done so many times before. There were three of us in the water, but I was the youngest of my cousins. There was a storm brewing that afternoon, but it was pleasantly warm as it had been all week and the water was fresh and inviting. None of us gave it a second thought. We just jumped in.

We weren't even halfway to the embankment when I realized that I couldn't reach the sand underneath me and the water was covering my head. I thought to myself if I can just push myself down to the sand and push myself up I can get air at the top. Pushing myself off the ocean floor worked for a while, but it was getting more and more difficult to reach the top. I don't know how long I had been doing this when I felt a sharp push from behind.

One of my uncles had jumped in to "rescue" me. I swallowed more water than on my own, but at least he got me out of the water and onto the shore. Almost drowning was scary. I didn't even know how to float. But I wasn't going to let fear dominate my life. I was determined never to go through this situation again. As soon as we got back home, I asked Dad to teach me how to swim.

The beauty of it was that I could learn to swim in a pool carved out of rock aside one of our fabulous beaches here in Australia. The rock pool was full of sea water. At the end of each swim session with Dad, he would ask me to inhale the sea water through my nose and then spit it out through my mouth. I know, it sounds disgusting, but it worked. It cleaned out my sinuses, and they never bothered me again.

After this memorable holiday, it was time to start High School. My parents had enrolled me in an all-girls Catholic High School as the education was designed to be more challenging than the average public high school. I wasn't fussed about God at this stage. I had learned to shut Him out and besides, I had my music now.

At this school, I would finally have friends. Girls that I could play with just as I did with my cousins. Others like me that were only interested in having fun and being silly. In my first year, we were all in the same class. That's how we got to know each other. We shared all the same classes.

Our small group consisted of girls of all different backgrounds. Carla was from Chile, Katrina's family was from Croatia. Nicola's family was from Italy, and Joanna's parents were from Poland. We all had one thing in common. We all had at least one parent that we felt didn't love us. Just as an example, Katrina's Dad was unkind to her because she was the first born and wasn't a boy. He had wanted a son. So he used to smack her a lot and yell at her a lot. Katrina had a younger brother. He treated Katrina's brother very differently, and this caused her pain.

Up until high school, I remember that I had been smacked a lot and yelled at a lot. But in truth, I don't remember learning anything from this except to be afraid, until one day you become numb to it and you no longer let it affect you. You know it is going to hurt physically, but you know you can get through it because you have done it many times before. It never taught me what I did wrong or why I shouldn't have done something. At least now I was in High School I was too big to be smacked. I had so much work to do for school that as long as I was studying hard, Mom was happy.

For all of these girls, their parents were the first of their family to come and live in Australia. They were the first generation of immigrants in Australia. I was the only one born in Australia. As I had such dark features, I didn't look Australian. So I fit right in because none of my friends looked Australian either.

It was wonderful to have friends at school finally. Friends I could talk to and spend time with, and we could study for exams together. Friends that understood me, and I understood them. I felt connected to these girls, just as I had done with my cousins. The incredible part was that I could see them every day. I didn't have to wait until it was the weekend to see them.

There were more people in the world just like me. Not beautiful, not ugly. We didn't stand out in any way. We weren't tall or short. Most of us just had brown hair. We weren't fat or skinny. We cared for each other, and we were happy when we were together. I felt supported when I was with them. It was comforting to know that I was not alone because there were others out there just like me.

Others that felt just like I did. They were good and had kind hearts, and this made them beautiful to me. We never said anything negative about each other. We talked about ourselves, and what we were going through and we never judged each other because we were all going through the same. Listening and sharing our stories and being very, very goofy together. Making up our games and living in our little world, where we were amazing in each other's eyes. We were happy together.

This year would be one of the most important years in my life. Not because I had started High School, but because my Dad had a major heart attack. He was only thirty-five years old. This event would rock my very foundation. The day we went to the hospital to visit him it was so painful for Dad to look at us, that he asked us to leave the room. He was the sole breadwinner now in our home. My Mom had stopped working the year before, and he was terrified. What would happen to us without him?

A few doors away from his ward, there was a waiting room. It had a piano in it. I played Mozart's Turkish Rondo for him in the hope that it would cheer him up. I played it over and over again because I knew that he liked this piece.

Years later I asked him if he had enjoyed it and he said that he didn't even hear it.

My thoughts at this time were that we never say "I love you" to each other. My Dad was dying of a broken heart because he didn't **know** that I loved him. Once we got back home, I told him every chance I could that I loved him. Dad's heart might have been broken in the first place because he didn't know that someone loved him. It never occurred to me that if he passed away, we would suffer financially. I did not understand what that meant. I just knew that if he were gone, I would be all alone because I no longer had Dad in my life.

My Dad was a workaholic. I asked him recently if he had any self-reproach and the only regret was that he didn't get to spend enough time with my sister and me because he was always working. I guess, as long as he had something to work on, his mind was distracted, and he didn't have to think. He was just focusing on the task at hand.

I see so many people working such long hours just to have more things because they believe that this material stuff will make them happy. In today's world, families need to have two or more cars, houses with many rooms. I challenge you to assess your life today. Think about what you can live without that wouldn't even be missed. Think about the last thing you bought that you thought you needed to have. An item that you thought would make you feel better or happier. How long did the joy of obtaining this item last? Then you're on to the next item. Buying more things is like filling up your stomach with water in the hope that you will stop feeling hungry. Don't be like my parents, in search of a "better" life.

Understand today that what you need is not out there. Finding your inner peace will not come from a material possession. It will come from doing this work with me in this book. Looking at your past and understanding the decisions you have made so far. Understanding who you think you are and realizing who you are for real. Slowly letting go of all the things you believe about yourself that are not true.

My Mom bought a beautiful set of china called Royal Doulton. It had roses and was very expensive. This stoneware sat in a cabinet for a special occasion for many years. We never used this set. My Mom ended up giving it away because it made her sad that we had all left home and never once enjoyed that beautiful set of plates. Does this sound like you: buying unique things for a special occasion? Being alive today reading this book is the special occasion. You are special just by being here. Every day you touch other people's lives and don't even realize it.

My Dad's heart attack was just the beginning of the end for my parents here in Australia. They finally had the beautiful home they had always dreamed of, but as I said, that is never enough.

The following year, my piano tutor enrolled me in a piano eisteddfod. I was so excited because I had played at numerous concerts for my teacher, but this was an actual competition. Back in those days, we would select a piece from the list and prepare that. On the day there would be various other students presenting that very same piece. There were no age restrictions. Did I say I was excited? I think excited was an understatement at the time. I could hardly wait.

We were performing in a massive hall in the City for the actual event. My group had thirty-two students playing the same musical score, and I was number twenty-four on the list. We sat in the audience waiting our turn. The first student played my piece, and I thought it was lovely, but they got the rhythm all wrong. Then the second child played and did the same thing.

After the fifth and sixth performance, I realized that they couldn't all be wrong. I opened up my music and looked carefully at the notes as the next person played. **My timing was all wrong!** My hands became so sweaty and cold. I could feel my heart throbbing so loudly in my throat I thought it was going to jump straight out of my mouth. What do I do?

I had spent months preparing this piece. Hours and hours just to get it right. There was no way I could just change it at the last minute. I wanted to go home. Please don't make me play. My parents were both with me, and they could see my angst. They had done so much for me to be here. I couldn't let them down. They had sacrificed so much for me. I had to go on.

My confidence was completely shattered after this event. It would take me over twenty years to recover from this incident. The tendons in my forearms began to ache after participating in this competition. My fingers felt like they had pins and needles in them and they hurt when I tried to play the piano or type on my typewriter. As the months progressed, I was having trouble holding objects in my hands. I didn't have the strength to carry them. Writing became impossible as I was finding it harder and harder to hold the pen. I was struggling to wash my hair and pretty much just get on with my life.

To make things worse, I had to have braces put on my teeth, so my mouth ached as well. I was not having fun. Not only that, but my canine on the left-hand side of my face had decided to grow into the roof of my mouth right at the back. I had to have an operation to tie a chain to this tooth and attach it to the rest of my braces so that they could gradually and painfully pull it towards the front of my mouth.

A memory I have of this time that I love is that when I came to from my operation, my Mom was sitting next to me. Who knows how long she had been sitting there waiting for me to wake up? I felt very sick from the anesthetic and couldn't stop vomiting, but felt comforted that my Mom was there. This moment made me feel that she cared for me. It was the first time I remember feeling loved by her. Her smile reassured me that everything would be alright and for a few short hours, it was just the two of us. It was nice to feel her love.

My parents took me to several doctors to see if they could find a cure for my hands, but they just told them that I needed an operation and there was no guarantee that it would work. From here on, the plan was to find a treatment that didn't involve surgery.

I was so angry at the world. How can I be given this love of music and then be denied the right to play? "That's it, God, I have had it with you! Why are you punishing me? Why do you keep singling me out? What have I done to deserve this? No matter what I do, it will never be good enough for you. I never want to speak to you again! Do you hear me? NEVER! I HATE YOU!"

Up until my 15th birthday, I got progressively worse. My parents took me to have acupuncture done to see if this would alleviate my pain. However, it was useless. Nothing helped. Meanwhile, they spoke to my relatives in Argentina, and they managed to track down a doctor that specialized in healing athletes and people involved in sports when they had problems with their joints or muscles. Apparently, he could help me without having an operation.

I had my 15th birthday here in Australia. It was lovely. I could invite my friends from school. So, Katrina, Carla, and Nicola attended. I was quite surprised that Mom allowed me to bring them so that they could be a part of my special day. Throughout school and high school, I couldn't go to sleepovers or even just go out with friends. The previous year was the only year I attended the school camp. As a result, this made the bond with my friends even stronger.

My Mom was very over-protective. She taught me that the world was not a safe place. I learned that all that mattered was our family, just the four of us. Mom, Dad, Anna and me. Everything else was external, and others could easily hurt you. My parents would never hurt me and were practically the only people I could trust in the world. I wasn't worried about not going to school events because we did many things with my cousins every weekend.

We visited beaches together and went to play in different parks. I got to see my friends at school every day, so it didn't bother me if I couldn't go out to the movies with them on the weekend. Now that I think of it, I don't remember ever going to any of my friends' birthdays either. It is better that my parents cared too much than that they didn't care at all. All things considered, I didn't feel that I missed out on anything important.

All through this, I had a huge crush on a boy. My first real crush. His name was Michael, and he was three years older than me. His parents had become close friends with my parents. Maybe because they also immigrated from Argentina. Just try and create a mental picture. He was so tall and so handsome and here I was, fifteen years old with glasses and braces. It didn't help much that I still looked twelve years old because my boobs hadn't kicked in yet, so my chest was still quite flat. Michael wasn't interested in me. I had liked him for over two years, and he didn't even notice that I was there. He had a different girlfriend every couple of months. Why wasn't I good enough to be one of those girls?

My parents never told us that we were pretty or beautiful or anything along those lines because they thought that we would get a big head and wouldn't be humble. To them, humility was more important than being narcissistic. The problem with this was, that because Michael didn't like me back, I assumed that it was because I was ugly. So it was a blessing that I would soon be leaving for Argentina. There was no point thinking about someone that doesn't know you even exist. Being beautiful wasn't ranked as something important in my house. If you thought you were beautiful, then you were vain.

Again, see how easy it is to believe something about yourself. In this case, it was because a boy wasn't interested in me. He didn't even say or do something to me to make me feel inadequate in any way. I deduced that I must be unattractive and that any partner I would have in my life would have to be smart so we could have something in common.

Thinking I was ugly is so funny because I've never been overweight, I'm not too tall, and not too short. I am so average and ordinary. My nose is not big, nor do I have big ears or anything that stands out that I would think there was something wrong with my appearance. My weight has always been in the middle, so I haven't been skinny either. I have loved exercising almost as much as reading, so I feel quite balanced in that sense. I've never had a hang up with my glasses, and even though the braces looked yucky, I knew they were temporary and would be coming off soon.

So it doesn't take much to decide something about yourself that doesn't serve you. That doesn't make you feel good about who you are. It can be as simple as that. I don't even remember ever having a conversation with Michael. The truth is that we had absolutely nothing in common. I also felt awkward because I attended an all-girls' school. We didn't have boys present every day, so it felt weird talking to them.

What do they even talk about when they chat? With my male cousins, there was no difference than with my female cousins, but they felt like siblings. We just talked about everything and anything. We never had an issue striking up a conversation.

Take time now to look at your life up until the age of fifteen and write down all the things you chose to believe about yourself. When you have finished, look carefully at this list.

Firstly, write down all the memories that you have between the ages of ten and fifteen years.

Write down the actual events. Then write down your interpretations of what happened.

Look carefully at what you have chosen to believe in this period of your life.

How many of these beliefs are true?

How many of these make you feel good about yourself?

If you are here reading this book, it is your time to create a new list.

Make a list of all the things you are good at today.

Make a list of all the things that are true about you today. Be honest with yourself.

Write down the things that feel authentic to you. All the things that you can read and feel that you truly believe about yourself. Each week take one of the things that you thought about yourself when you were a child that did not make you feel good about yourself and tell yourself the opposite.

For example: if you believed that you weren't pretty.

Start telling yourself how beautiful you are now.

Look at the things that are attractive about you.

Do you have long, slender legs? Do you have beautiful hands?

Are your eyes beautiful? Stop to look at the pattern in your eyes when the light hits them. Eyes are quite amazing, and everyone's pupils are unique to them, therefore making you a one of a kind.

Do you like your hair or is your smile dazzling?

Make a list of what you think is beautiful about you right now and add to that list as the days go on. Try to think of beauty as you would a sunset or a flower. Not the beauty you see in magazines.

Try to look in your eyes so that you can see your spirit, rather than just looking at your outer shell.

Chapter 4

THE PURPOSE OF YOUR RELATIONSHIPS

Here I was, fifteen years old and back in Argentina living with my Aunt Rebecca. Mom and Dad stayed behind in Australia with Anna, because they needed to sell our house. I was sent to Argentina soon after my 15th birthday because they wanted me to start my treatment with the sports doctor as soon as possible.

The pain in my wrists was intolerable by now, and my hands had lost all strength. My doctor started me off with cortisone injections. It seemed like every week I was having different tests done, or different drugs were given to me to see if they worked. I felt like a guinea pig in a lab. After a year of treatment, I was feeling better. Not healed, because the pain was still there, but the strength was coming back to my hands. The cortisone injections had made me blow up like a balloon. All in all, I had gained twelve kilograms in the first three months of being in Argentina.

My Dad arrived first after my parents sold their house. He came to buy a home for all of us so that when Mom and Anna arrived, we would have a place to live. In the meantime, my

Mom and my sister were living with Sofia and her family in Australia.

During these first few months, my cousin was dating a boy from across the road. My cousin was just a year older than me. Her parents suspected that she was dating this boy, but she told them that she was leaving early every morning because I was the one seeing this boy. She didn't want to get into trouble. Neither of us could date boys yet. We were too young. My Dad didn't say anything even though I swore that it wasn't true.

One morning I asked my Dad why he didn't stand up for me when he knew that I was telling the truth. I'll never forget what he said to me that day. He stated that he knew who I was and that he didn't need to prove anything to anybody else. I was confused at the time because I thought your loved ones were supposed to defend you. That's what Mom would have done. At the time, I felt that I couldn't rely on him.

How could he let them say those things about me? I felt like they were saying I was a slut and he didn't care that they thought that about me. At the time, I felt so alone, like if something terrible happened, I was on my own to sort it out. Feeling that I was on my own made me afraid because I didn't know if I had the skills to stand up for myself if the time came.

Now, I realize it was the loveliest thing he has ever said to me. He was saying that he knew who I was and what I was capable of and that nothing else mattered to him. To be honest, he didn't care what they thought because that could not change who I was to him.

Once my parents arrived in Argentina, and we settled into our new home, we had the final visit with this doctor. He said that his conclusion was that most of the illness was in my mind. "Is he insane? Did he just say that I made this whole thing up? But the pain was real?" I felt like he stated that I had wasted everyone's time concocting such an elaborate story.

With what intention: to get attention? I was angry with this doctor because he hadn't completely cured me and now I thought he was saying that I had made it all up, to justify that he couldn't fix me. He was blaming me for not being able to do his job properly. I was furious with this man. "How dare he say that to me?"

The truth is that he was right. I had created the pain in my hands and my wrists. It was not because I felt that I needed to get anyone's attention, but to protect myself from having to play piano in front of anyone else ever again. To protect myself from ever having to feel the humiliation I felt at that competition. How could I be the only one to have played it incorrectly? I cannot express in words the embarrassment I felt. Although, I'm pretty sure my parents could hear my heart shatter into a million pieces on that stage that day.

I attended a private school for my first year in Argentina. It was supposed to be an English-speaking school. I thought we were going to learn the subjects in English, but that was not the case. The teenagers here were of very wealthy families. These upper-class teenagers were very snotty, and they thought they were above everyone else. Not quite what I was accustomed to in my life. I missed my friends that I left behind in Australia and I would write to them often. Needless to say, I did not make any friends in this new school.

I felt at the end of my first year that I hadn't gained enough knowledge to move on to the next grade. The subjects were so different to Australia. We were learning physics and chemistry and philosophy. These topics were incredible. I wanted to know more. I wanted to know them better.

Unfortunately, with private schools, they don't care if you don't learn in class because they just assume that you will hire a private tutor outside of school. My parents decided to send me to a private tutor after this first year, and I kept seeing him for the first eight months of the next grade to help me stay on top of things.

The following year, my parents enrolled me in a private Catholic High School. I sat in class for one hour and walked home. I told my parents that if they didn't send me to an ordinary public school, I would walk home from this school every day. They couldn't force me to stay there. I wanted to learn and not be surrounded by snobs with attitudes. It felt like such a waste of money to me. I loved the public system, and Argentina was no different.

By this stage, my hands were much better because I wasn't thinking about them anymore. My parents decided to buy me a piano so that I could play whenever I wanted. I didn't have to go to lessons. We went to a piano shop in the City, and I fell in love with a black piano. I just loved everything about it. I adored the look of it. How it felt under my fingertips. Even the smell of it was divine. But the owner of the shop told us that it was sold and was awaiting delivery. I stood up and looked around, but nothing else interested me. So we left.

The following afternoon, I arrived home from school to find the removalists there with the black piano I had seen the day before. Apparently, the person that had ordered it lived in an apartment on the fifth floor and the staircase was too narrow for them to get the piano up there. As this person hadn't paid for it yet, here they were, delivering it to me. I have had so many of these moments where an outcome feels like it is destiny. I've also had many not meant to be moments, and one of these was just around the corner.

In this same year, my cousins Maria and Christopher came to visit Argentina. They came with their cousins Sonia and Paul. I had grown up with these two cousins as well and always loved them as if they were my real relatives. We could see Sonia and Paul, but we weren't allowed to see Maria and Christopher.

Not having permission to see Maria and Christopher broke my heart. Why couldn't I see them again? It may be the last time. I held this grudge with my mom for many, many years thinking that she was the one that didn't give them permission to see us. I was so angry with my mom. How could she keep us apart when she knew how much we loved each other?

My aunt and uncle weren't talking to my parents. The grown-ups had all had a falling out before my parents left for Argentina. What was the reason they were upset with each other? I don't know and don't think it matters. The fact is that many years later I discovered that it was my aunt who didn't allow them to visit us and not the other way around. I thought it was strange that Sonia and Paul could come to see us, but not Maria and Christopher.

This year was turning out to be awesome. I was finally doing well in school and mastering all the subjects. I was enjoying the science subjects. At the end of this year, we had to sit our end of year exams. I joined a study group with three other students from my class, and we each took turns to study at each other's house for six weeks leading up to the exams.

Now, this was amusing. We were two girls and two boys in the group. The other girl in our group was called Daniela. The boys were Luke and George. Daniela had a huge crush on George. She just adored him and was so excited that we were all going to be working closely together for the next six weeks getting ready to ace these exams. I had spent this whole year wishing I had a boyfriend. I felt it was time for me to know what it was like to hold someone's hand and have my first kiss and all that.

After our third week of studies, we were all walking home from Daniela's house. Daniela and George stayed back chatting, and Luke and I got to talking ahead. I thought they were going to hook up. As for Luke, I had nothing in common with him and found it awkward to talk to him. I just wasn't at ease at all. As a result, everything I said felt like a polite conversation. Like talking to a stranger on a bus. I found him attractive enough, but we just had nothing to say. I couldn't wait for this walk to be over. It seemed like forever.

The weeks progressed, and something just happened with George. It just all fell into place effortlessly. We fell in love. There was so much in common with him. We could talk for hours, and it felt so comfortable to talk to him about anything. I was confused. I mean, Daniela was gorgeous. The moment he came to kiss me, I asked him if he got the right girl. He laughed. I didn't want to betray her. Daniela had known George for several years. They had known each other since primary school, and I felt like I was butting in.

He assured me that he had no feelings for her and he felt awkward around her. Just like I was with Luke, not sure what to discuss. He said they had nothing in common and I could relate to that. I was thrilled because he was smart and warm and funny. I didn't notice him because I thought he belonged to someone else. It was evident to me that he was better suited to Daniela. He was two years older than me, and his family was originally from Greece.

It was wonderful. We could talk for hours and never run out of anything to say to each other. I felt that just like my Dad belonged to my Mom, that I finally had someone that belonged to me. My own love. I didn't find him physically attractive. He was quite stocky and robust. I had always dreamed of a tall, slender man.

George had a flat chest, which I thought was quite odd. I thought all men had chests just like my Dad and my uncles. I never noticed, until I started dating George, that some men have flat chests. He was the same height as me, which was not very tall for a man. His legs were so chunky and muscular.

His hair was curly and thick, I mean the curls were tight. But he made up for all this with his gorgeous brown eyes and amazing smile. I would spend hours staring into his eyes.

We spent the first six months inseparable. We couldn't stop kissing when we were together. This relationship was true love. I couldn't stop thinking about him when we were apart, and I couldn't wait to see him again. Of course, we saw each other every day as we were still going to school together.

We went to the same high school for the next couple of years. I thought George was my knight in shining armor. The **one** that would complete me so that I would never feel that anything was missing ever again. He would never discard me. I would feel cared for with him. I would feel important and protected. Because of George, I would finally feel seen and heard.

At the time I felt so lucky that of all the girls, he had chosen me. After fifteen months, I decided that it was safe to have sex with him. I was sure that this wasn't a one night stand and that he wouldn't just take off. This was true love. In church, we had learned that you only give your virginity away when you get married. But I wasn't planning on ever talking to God again, so in reality, I had nothing to lose.

I understood that your virginity was something you gave to someone special and that it is your gift to them. Panic set in once I had given it away. What if George did decide that he didn't want me anymore? Or if he chose to walk away after a few months? What if he got bored with me? I had nothing left to give to anyone else. Fear took over. I spent the next three months crying and telling him that he was going to dump me because I had nothing left to give him. He had no reason to stay with me. I was jealous of any girl that came to talk to him because they were all a potential threat.

I felt insecure all the time now. My insecurity stemmed from the fact that George was so much smarter than me and that he would eventually grow bored with me. What would take me four hours to understand, he learned in one hour. He focused intensely on the task at hand and just nailed it every time. The bottom line was that I didn't feel good enough to be with him. So everything felt like a personal attack.

His parents didn't like me. I mean, how could they? Anything they said made me feel that I shouldn't be there because their son was too good to be with me. He deserved someone better, someone smarter, someone prettier.

Eventually, George's parents got divorced, and I realized that many of the things that were said, were never really about me at all. They were just talking about themselves and their pain. I took it personally because I thought that I didn't belong there. I felt that I wasn't worthy of George's time and love.

Having said that, his grandfather was so lovely to me. He was so kind, and he would tell me all these wonderful stories of how they had emigrated from Greece and how he had met George's grandmother. I wish I had a grandfather just like him when I was growing up. As George was an only child, we spent a lot of time with his grandparents. His grandparents' house was the one place that I felt accepted.

George's mother was brilliant. Elena was so slim and beautiful. She was so talented in the kitchen that she made delicious, sweet cakes for a bakery in the City. Apparently, Elena's Dad was so strict that he wouldn't let her do anything. She wasn't allowed out with friends or to go out after she got home from school. This strict upbringing forced her to marry George's father quite young, just to leave home and have some freedom. George's father was a chef in a restaurant.

At this point, all I could think about was George. I didn't care about anything else. He was the first person to notice me. The first person that looked at me and I could look back at him without being punished because he belonged to me. It took about a year before I could say that I loved him to his face. I was afraid that it would put too much pressure on the relationship, but it turned out, that he said it back, and for a while, everything was perfect.

Once I started having sex and my parents were aware of this, my Mom started giving me relationship tips. For example, it is the woman's job to keep the man happy. It was my duty to provide sex whenever George wanted it. Otherwise, he would look for it elsewhere. So sex, felt like an obligation, like a chore at times, because I felt I couldn't say no. The only times I would have a break was during my periods. So technically, it was the woman's fault if the man cheated because we didn't keep them satisfied.

Sex was not something you enjoyed or something that gave you any gratification. For us women, it was a job we had to do if we loved our men. I didn't know what I was missing out on until we watched porn movies with George and I learned about masturbation. At least, after George finished having sex with me, I could go to the bathroom and pleasure myself. Masturbating felt like such a solitary act. He got to use my body to get what he needed, and I had to go and relieve myself on my own.

It didn't seem fair, and it was not something that gave me any joy at all. Often I cried because it felt like such a selfish thing to do to someone that you love, and I felt used, but I never said a word about it. I worried that if I complained or said anything about it that he would leave and find someone that would be happy with him just the way he was.

The second thing I learned from Mom, was that it is our job to fix our partners. If they are struggling with any addictions or bad habits or anything else that we didn't like, it was the woman's job to change them. This concept is by far the funniest thing

I have ever learned. When George wouldn't change his mind about something, it made me feel that my love was broken. I couldn't get him to see my way. I couldn't fix him. My love wasn't strong enough to make it all better.

I was always comparing our relationship to others. Every time we watched a film, I would start to question our relationship because it didn't measure up to the one in the movie. I'd spend many days finding fault with George and how he treated me in comparison. Frequently comparing our relationship would be the cause of many arguments between us.

A problem emerged with this relationship that I had not been aware of beforehand. When George did something that I didn't like or that upset me, I wouldn't say anything. I think it was the fear that he would leave and not want to be with me anymore. Often, years later from an incident, we would be arguing, and I would burst out with all these accumulated grudges from way back because I had been holding onto all of them. All this junk was festering inside of me because I was too scared to speak up.

Because I loved him so much, I trusted him with my innermost secrets, believing that it was safe to do so. Sharing my secrets included my Mom discarding me at five years old. He took it on as his duty to protect me from this woman who brought me into the world but didn't care about me. As we were both just studying and neither of us was working yet, we were always at my house. So tension began to grow between George and my parents.

Mom and Dad were protecting my little sister who was only a young teenager at the time. She didn't need to be seeing her older sister having sex at such a young age. They probably weren't that comfortable with us having sex under their roof, but we had nowhere else to go.

Eventually, George's parents divorced, and he became

more and more possessive. He was so angry with his Dad. His Dad had fallen in love with another woman from the restaurant where he worked. When his parents finally separated, he talked for hours about his Dad. I just listened. At the end of his rant, he looked at me with so much anger and asked me why I had nothing to say. I remember saying that he would always be his Dad. That he had made mistakes, but that it didn't change the fact that he would always be his father, no matter how angry George was at this moment.

I felt like I always had to choose between George and my family. I was frequently crying. What they didn't know, was that I had been on the contraceptive pill for over a year now. I started using the contraceptive pill George's mother was on. We didn't want to see a doctor because we were too embarrassed. Little did I know at the time the effects that this can have on your body, and more importantly, the devastating impact it can have on your mind because of the hormones fluctuating.

Gradually I felt myself slipping further and further into an abyss. How do you run away from yourself? It was George's job to save me. I thought that for once in my life someone would see me and through them, I would be able to accept myself. That for once in my life I could feel loved for who I am and through them, would be able to love myself as well. I've never felt such loneliness in all my life, and yet a lot of people surrounded me at the time. Darkness was starting to envelop me. I never felt so alone and so separate from everyone and everything.

It was at this point in my life that my parents asked me if I wanted to take up piano lessons again. My Dad was doing renovations for a piano teacher, and she came highly recommended. My parents felt that I needed something else to focus on and they were right. They had watched me go from a confident, bright, young girl to an insecure, withdrawn, clingy teenager.

I agreed to have piano lessons and consequently, met one of the most amazing piano teachers I would meet on my journey. Her name was Elisa. She taught me so many valuable things that I could use if I were ever to teach piano. We had hourly lessons. The first thirty minutes we learned theory and rhythm exercises. I have never had a rhythm problem since. The second half we dedicated to piano playing. Now, this was mind blowing to me. Elisa introduced me to the greatest composers of all time from the very first lesson.

Elisa taught me the concept that I love you, but I don't really like you right now. If I wasted one full week without practicing, she was disappointed and would get cross with me. Music was her life. So she couldn't understand how you could spend one day without practice, let alone one whole week. I started to believe in my ability to play through her faith in me. She made me feel that anything was possible.

She taught me so much about technique and working with curved fingers and that playing a million scales has no value at all if the way you play is all over the shop. The only thing we never focused on was dynamics, and this is what gives music its color.

Later on, in my playing, people would comment that my playing had no feeling and this could have been attributed to two things. Firstly, I dreaded playing for others because they may judge all my mistakes, and secondly, I played without dynamics, so everything sounded the same. Dynamics means playing softly and loudly and changing the intensity of the sound.

Our lessons would start off with Bach (absolute genius when it came to technical work). Here I would teach the left hand to be as good as the right. The second book would be

Mozart, Haydn or Beethoven. Again more technical work, but we always had one sonata going. Then there was Chopin, and my real love of music took off here. I was more in love than I had ever been. How did I not know of this composer? When I could master his pieces, I could feel my soul soar to unimaginable heights. The feeling of playing his waltzes alone was bliss. I could spend hours just playing his works.

Beethoven took emotion to a whole other level. His sonatas are sublime. I gradually went from one hour a day to two hours a day. I didn't do anything else outside of school, so two hours of playing the piano weren't much. For a while it was wonderful. I was playing better than ever because I was just learning for me. On weekends, I could easily play three to four hours.

I was finally ready to start University. I almost dropped out and didn't even finish high school because I had a philosophy teacher that I disliked in my final year and I didn't make it through her subject. You need to pass all subjects to finish high school. I couldn't see the use of this topic. What a waste of time. Eventually, I knuckled down, spent hours in the library and graduated. I found it so interesting that I considered changing my course and learn psychology instead. But I didn't.

So off I went to study chemistry and prove what a brainiac I truly was. I enjoyed the learning process. Chemistry is quite amazing. It shows you how things work. I especially loved the work in the lab and learning about the world we were living in, especially when viewed from underneath a microscope. You get to see the universe in a whole new light when you study it from a chemical point of view.

In this same year, my piano teacher had signed us all up to play at a recital. We were in a huge hall, playing on a grand piano in front of at least 200 people. My piano teacher was part of a music school that had eight teachers in total. Most of them had studied together in their youth and decided when they finished all their education, to start a music school between them. This school was not part of the Music Conservatorium in Argentina.

So on the day of this recital, we had eight different teachers presenting their top ten students. Add to this all the parents and relatives that were allowed to attend. This concert was a massive event. I was pretty sure that I wasn't ready for this yet. My heart was pounding so hard in my chest that I thought it would come leaping out of my mouth at any moment. My hands were sweating profusely, and I just couldn't stop shaking. The blood was draining out of my cheeks, and I was starting to feel dizzy.

Why was I doing this to myself again? Why did I let my teacher talk me into this? I'm all for facing your fears, but this is ridiculous. Maybe I would never get over this fear. I just wanted to run right out of there and never return. Escaping right now meant letting Elisa down. She believed in me more than anything. What did my piano teacher see in me? Always telling all her younger students how wonderfully I played, but I couldn't see it. Elisa thought I was amazing, and never missed an opportunity to tell me so, and here I was, struggling to breathe.

George was there with me backstage waiting for me to go on. I never confessed to him what happened at that dreadful eisteddfod. It wasn't important or relevant to our relationship. I wanted to erase that moment in time from my life and wished it had never happened. Never wanting to talk about it or even remembering that it had occurred. Placing it at the furthest point in the back of my mind, so I didn't have to think about it. He didn't have a clue what I was going through that evening.

Mom, Dad, and Anna were in the audience waiting to see me play. I was trying so hard to pretend that everything was okay and that it was not a problem. They called my name. Somehow, I managed to get to the piano, sit down, and prop my book up on the piano stand. I felt alone, and everyone's eyes were staring at me. After a few minutes, I placed my fingers on the keys. Nothing. My fingers wouldn't move. I couldn't breathe. It felt like someone was suffocating me. They had their hands wrapped around my neck, and they were gently squeezing, tighter and tighter.

I looked at the page. Nothing. Nothing on the page looked familiar. What do I do? Getting up and walking off the stage seemed appealing, but somehow, not the right thing to do. I tried to play the first line of my Bach piece. Blank. My mind went blank. I couldn't think at all. It felt like I had been sitting there for days. Suddenly, my fingers started to play. As a result, my fingers felt like a wind-up toy, completely on autopilot. I had no control of my hands at all. They were just doing all the work for me. I could hear clapping, which meant, I must have finished performing.

It would be years before I attempted to sit an exam or perform in front of an audience again. I thought I was going to have a heart attack due to this event. My heart had never beaten that fast in its entire life. It was a miracle I didn't pass out or end up in the hospital. Most of all, I had let down my teacher. I couldn't remember how well or how badly I had played and had no recollection of what I had done.

As much as I thought I was facing my fear, it felt like a disaster at the time since I couldn't remember any of it. Maybe, this was something that was not meant to be. It seems as though, the more I tried to overcome this wretched fear, the further away I got from conquering it. While I overcame my fear of the water by learning to swim, performance anxiety would take a lot more work and patience.

My parents didn't want my sister or me to work until we had finished our studies. To them, this was their priority, so that we could have the best chance at having a prosperous life. By the time I was twenty years old, my Dad had approached me about whether I was on the contraceptive pill. He told me of the effects that it can have on your body and that my mom couldn't use it because it messed with her hormones. It was after this chat that I decided to get off these drugs, and we would just have to figure out another way to have sex with George without falling pregnant.

My Mom also talked about how we sacrifice the things that we love, for the people we love. She said that she used to love dancing, but as my Dad didn't like dancing, she decided to give it up. Love was about compromise, about putting those we love first. Therefore, later in life, as a mom, I would be last on the list just as she was. My Dad came first, then her daughters. Her needs were last, and that was how it should be. This is what love looked like in my home.

We learn so much about ourselves through our relationships. Who we are and what we are capable of doing. Sometimes, relationships push us to be the best that we can be. Other times, it shows us that we have the skills to do horrible things. We all have it in us to choose love or to choose hatred. To do good deeds or cruel acts that will harm others.

Due to the choices we make, we define who we are. Are we a caring, loving parent or are we harsh and abusive towards our children? Do we treat our partners with love and understanding or do we treat them like they are not worthy of our time and they are beneath us?

In each moment, we are choosing who we want to be. Often, we need to experience the opposite to know that we do not wish to be *that*. Rather, having lived through an experience, we are aware we could never do that to another human being. While others can't help but follow tradition, because it happened to them, they, therefore, pass on this behavior as normal and acceptable. If it was good enough for them, then it must be good enough for others.

I urge you to look carefully at this time in your life.

Make a note of all your relationships.

Who are they in relation to you?

Write down what you have learned about yourself from these relationships.

What did you believe at that time about yourself and the other person?

What do you feel was the purpose of this relationship in your life?

LEARNING FROM YOUR MISTAKES

The following year I was a bit of a mess. All the feuding at home and the constantly having to choose a side was driving me insane. Aunt Lucy visited us from Australia, and I begged her to please take me back with her. So after she finished visiting her mom in Argentina, I left my parents to go live with Aunt Lucy in Australia. It wasn't long before I was living with my cousin Sofia and her family instead.

This period of my life was memorable to me. After years of fighting back at home, I had almost fifteen months of peace. My cousin and I shared a room, and I would keep her up for hours at night talking to her. As she had to work a nine to five job as a dental nurse, I didn't get to see her during the day, and so we had a lot of catching up to do when she got home.

My aunt and uncle were kind enough to let me have a piano in their house so I could practice. This year was a magical time for me because I felt loved and felt full of love for them. I helped with the cooking and the housework whenever it was possible. I spent my days looking for a job, but being straight out of high school and with no experience or work skills, this was quite difficult. Aunt Paula had a few cleaning jobs throughout the week, and I would go with her to help out. This time together made us bond. We were finally talking to each other as adults.

I loved my Aunt Paula very much and wished so much that she could have been my real mom. Mom and I never had these conversations. I felt heard, and she made me feel that I mattered. My Uncle Peter was fantastic too. He treated me like another daughter. There weren't any moments when I lived with them, that I felt out of place or unwanted or that I wasn't just one more daughter to them. They treated me as an equal in their home. These few months made me the happiest I had been in a long time.

Towards the end of the year, though, George's grandfather passed away, and my Dad started having heart problems again. So my Mom asked me to please come home, and I did. My Dad ended up having a major heart attack. He had an operation for them to repair the damage. Apparently, the artery that had a blockage was called the "Widow Maker." We were lucky that they caught it in time and the doctors could mend his heart.

After my return, I spent months looking for George's grandfather when we visited his house. His grandmother was still alive, so it felt weird seeing her but not him. One night, he visited me in a dream. I felt that he came to say good-bye. He let me know that he was alright and that he was happy. We had a huge conversation by a sparkling lake. The sun kept making the water shimmer. It felt like the chats we used to have when he was alive. I was at peace the next morning and knew that one day I would see him again. More importantly, I knew that he was okay.

Six months later, George proposed and we became engaged. I felt at the time that this was a desperate attempt to keep me happy so that I wouldn't leave again. Now, this is where I would like to talk about growing up receiving presents in my home. If you were good, you received what you wanted on special occasions, like Christmas or your birthday. Not being good, meant not receiving what you wanted because you obviously didn't deserve it.

The gift had to be beautifully wrapped, otherwise not enough thought and love went into it. In my childhood, love was measured by the gift you received. If someone loves you, they should know what you want. They know exactly what to do or what to give you to make you happy. That is what real love is, and this is what I grew up with in my home. How can the other person not know what you want? Don't they love me enough to give me what I need? Am I not worth enough to them to make an effort to get me the right gift?

The day George gave me my engagement ring, I was devastated. Firstly, it was nothing like what I had imagined my whole life, and secondly, he told me that his mother had chosen it and bought it for him. Wasn't I good enough for him to spare one hour of his precious time to go to a jeweler and pick out a ring for me? I felt betrayed. He buys me the wrong ring, and he made no effort whatsoever to purchase it. No love had gone into my engagement ring. It seemed like he was saying "Here's your ring, now leave me alone."

After six years of putting him first! This yucky engagement ring was the thanks I got. He might as well have slapped me in the face. It would have stung less. You see, I believed that putting George first was an act of love. Putting his needs first, his desires, his dreams. He was more important than I was. My dreams and desires weren't important enough, at least not compared to his.

After this event, I remember sitting in my class at University. I was studying chemistry at the time. I had chosen a difficult subject thinking that this would prove my intelligence and therefore earn my place by George's side. As I sat there, looking at my ring, I thought, I shouldn't need to have a degree from University to be good enough for anyone. I should be good enough just as I am. I wanted someone to love me for **who** I was, not **what** I was. It was all the same to me if he was a doctor or not. Most of all, I just wanted to be with him. When he wasn't squabbling with my parents, we played cards with each other, watched movies, and in general had a lot of fun together.

I enjoyed learning, but I couldn't imagine myself in a lab all day working with test tubes and mixing chemicals. It just wasn't me. The only constant in my life had been music. Growing up, each year I had wanted to be something different. For some years I wanted to be a veterinarian, for other years I wanted to be a lawyer. Then a scientist, a college professor, the list goes on. I enjoyed learning so much that I wanted to be everything, even a librarian. I couldn't make up my mind. But music had never changed. I never outgrew music.

My very first job in Argentina was for an Italian boss. It was an office job. I had to learn how to do all the tasks required of an office assistant. I learned to type letters, send mail, answer phone calls, do filing and run errands. I lasted one week. I didn't even wait for the pay.

He screamed at me all day. I think his volume switch was broken. For the most part, my boss didn't know how to speak calmly and explained things in a harsh manner. He yelled at me for everything, and he looked so stressed out. Hence, by the end of the week, I was a nervous wreck and Mom told me to leave. It wasn't worth the effort. For this reason, I am eternally grateful. My parents never forced me to stay in a job just for the money. They believed that work is something to be enjoyed seeing we spend most of the day there.

All things considered, my parents did a brilliant job. My cousins were being told to stick to one job because the money was the most important aspect. However, my parents taught me that it's okay to walk away from a job that makes you unhappy.

Of course, it's important to earn a living, but being completely miserable doing something for eight hours a day made no sense to Mom and Dad. This view on life was another instance in which my parents thought differently to everyone else around them. This piece of advice has always been something I have loved so much about my parents.

After that, I started working at a school to teach English. I finally had some money coming in. It was barely enough to cover the cost of the bus fair and my lunches. Mom and Dad didn't ask for any help with paying board or anything like that. So it seemed like I would never be able to get ahead to have a life of my own and eventually have a house to raise my own family. I even tried teaching English at home privately in my spare time, but it wasn't enough.

In between all the chaos at home and my life here in Argentina, we had many weekends with my Aunt Rita and Uncle Tony and my cousins. We spent hours playing cards at their house. These games would go well into the wee hours of the morning. It was normal for us to arrive home on a Sunday morning after two in the morning. These were my golden years.

These were the years we created our happiest memories in Argentina. But then my Mom had a fall out with my aunt, and we stopped visiting, and they stopped talking to each other. I say they because George and I would still visit my relatives at least once a month, but it was not the same. I missed them so much.

At this time, I gradually started to sink into a depression. My situation was hopeless. There was nothing to look forward to in my future. I hated my life and my place in the world. Everyone was endlessly bickering about nothing at all. My soul partner was supposed to complete me.

This expression is absurd because it implies that we are not whole as we are and therefore need someone else to be happy and feel fulfilled. I thought about suicide for months. Trying to work out the best way to check out. For the most part, I kept saying to God to just end it for me. Not even having the energy to take my own life, (yes, I was that desperate, that I was talking to God again!)

For months I spent my time trying to work out the best way to end my life. My situation was hopeless. There was no way out. Nothing was worth waking up every morning with a knot in my stomach and crying myself to sleep every night. I was fed up with the constant, futile battles between my partner and my parents. If I were gone, it would be over. There would be nothing to fight over. The pain would be gone. At least my pain.

My parents took me to see a psychologist. I talked to him for about two hours. At the end of our session, he said that the person that needed his help was George. Great! One more person that didn't want to waste time talking to me. After my visit to the psychologist, I packed a suitcase with my bare essentials, placed it under my bed, and thought about nothing but leaving for Australia.

I didn't want to be here anymore. If I could get away, my problems would all disappear. In Australia, I could have a satisfying job, make decent money, and live the life of my dreams. There would be no choosing between my parents and George anymore because there is no way they would all want to come to Australia with me.

It was at this time in my life that Aunt Lucy came to visit Argentina again. She came quite regularly to see her Mom as she was elderly and frail. I begged her to take me with her, and she asked my parents. They knew that I was miserable and agreed because they couldn't stand to see me cry anymore. I desperately wanted to get away and have a life away from all this drama. Not knowing who I was before my relationship with George, now I was even more lost and confused. All my thoughts had revolved around what he wanted, what he liked, what he needed and what I had to do to please him.

My predominant thoughts throughout my relationship with George were that he wouldn't love me anymore and would break up with me because I believed that he was too good for me and didn't deserve to be with him. Who else was going to want me now? I was used, second-hand, damaged goods. Rejected.

In George's defense, he never said he was better than me. He never stated that I wasn't worthy of his love. He never mentioned that I wasn't good enough to be with him. Not deserving to be with George was all concocted in my head. I had decided all this on my own. The intention of my story was never to blame or trash anyone else. It is to show you, how your predominant thoughts in every given moment produce certain outcomes.

Here I was now, suitcase in hand, off to have one of my best adventures yet: **independence!** I felt free and full of possibilities again. Away from all the sarcastic remarks and ongoing guilt trips and having to choose who to love today. I could focus on building a life together with my partner here in Australia.

This time I stayed with Aunt Lucy. My cousin Sofia was getting ready to marry, and it was all too crazy at their house now, and besides Aunt Lucy lived on her own. Exactly one month after arriving in Australia, I landed a job near the City and was on my way. How lucky was that, to find a job so soon with no office experience? I was working full time as a receptionist at a printing company.

I could breathe again. No more fighting, no more choosing sides. Clean slate. I was talking to George as often as possible. After all, we were still engaged, and we made a decision together to start a new life here in Australia, just the two of us. I was furious with my parents because I thought that they were the adults and they should know better than to have put me into this situation in the first place.

My anger with them was because they did not respect who I wanted to spend the rest of my life with after all, shouldn't this be my choice? I was also upset because for the longest time it seemed like they didn't care and now that someone wanted me, they didn't want to let me go. They decided that the person I had chosen wasn't good enough for me. This rage would eat away at me for the next ten years.

Living with my Aunt was no picnic because she was always in and out of doctors. She always had something wrong with her and loved talking about her diseases and how unwell she was. I guess this gave her the attention she needed after living by herself for such a long time.

Aunt Lucy always had dinner ready for me when I got home from work. She always asked me what I wanted for dinner the following day. We agreed to $50 board a week to help her with the bills, and we'd watch television together before going to sleep. It was nice having someone look after me while I was away from Mom and Dad for the first time in my life. The last time I had visited Australia and lived with my cousin Sofia, felt more like a holiday.

I would spend the weekends with my cousins Sofia and Isabella and my aunt and uncle. Sofia and her husband bought a house together with her parents, so it felt like old times. I just had a new cousin to play with now. Overall, I didn't want to be at my Aunt Lucy's house during the week. I felt that I had a second chance at life now. Talking about death and diseases seemed like a waste of time at this point in my life. I wanted to live!

So, I spent many nights working back late at my new job. I knew that the company didn't pay overtime, but I felt obligated to make up for all the lost time during the day while I was learning and making mistakes. These errors cost the company time and money. One of the directors always worked back as well. It seemed like he didn't want to go home either and I was incredibly fortunate that he respected me for being a hard worker and was an honorable man. He did his work, and I did mine. He felt like a dad to me. Always looking out for me and watching over me. Thus, making me feel protected.

With my new job, I was gaining new skills. Learning to talk to people over the phone. Completing many office chores like filing, photocopying, faxing, etc. which were all new to me. It felt like I was accomplishing something. I was helping others and learning new things. Meanwhile, I was getting paid to do all this cool stuff.

One person, I was so grateful to be working with was Sarah. I had never met anyone like her. I mean, she was beautiful. She was tall, slender, caramel skin, dark eyes, and dark hair. She looked like a model, in fact, I'm not sure what she was doing there. She should have been on the catwalk. But regardless of her external beauty, she was fantastic.

Through Sarah, I learned the meaning of patience. I could go up to her and ask her the same question a hundred times, and each time she would explain it as if it were the first time. Never moaning or groaning or telling me that she had already shown me how to do it. She never got flustered or frustrated with me. I couldn't believe it. She would stop whatever she was doing every single time just to help me learn something. To me, Sarah was stunning and kind. A winner combination.

We would spend our lunch time's playing cards. There were four of us in the office that would gather around Sarah's desk to eat lunch and play together. I love playing cards. It is such a wonderful way to interact with others. You look at each other, you laugh, and you talk. It is one of my favorite ways to socialize. You learn so much about others through playing games, and you are connecting to one another.

I spent one year living with my Aunt Lucy, but then Christmas was coming, and I knew George would have a break over the Christmas holidays from University, and he would want to come and visit me here in Australia. So, I searched for a separate apartment, as we would want to have some privacy when he came. The plan was for George to finish his University studies and come live with me in Australia. He was studying to become a doctor.

Throughout the year, I had spent most of my pay on all the things we would need in our new place. Towels, linen, plates, cups, all the necessities. I forgot two crucial details: furniture and appliances. So just before he arrived, I went to a large store and bought a sofa, tables and chairs, the fridge and my bed on credit. I had to get the bare essentials as I was on one wage to pay for everything on my own. I rented a one bedroom apartment to prepare for his visit.

We had six wonderful weeks to be together, just us. I enjoyed every minute we got to spend together. No fighting. No bickering. Most of all, no sarcastic comments. Unfortunately, George had to go back to Argentina to continue studying for the next two years. He wanted to complete a Master's degree or something that required extra time. I didn't care what it was. I was getting rather tired of waiting for him to finish whatever it was that he felt he needed to complete for us to start making a life together.

This year would turn out to be an incredibly exciting year for me. A much younger man started working at our company, and he was very loving and caring. We almost had an affair together, not because I found him physically attractive but because I saw so much of myself in him. Desperately longing to feel loved, to feel wanted. Actually, to feel anything that wasn't rejection and unworthiness.

George had left, and I was so sad to see him go. It left a

hole inside of me. An emptiness that I had never experienced before in my life. A part of me wanted to go back to Argentina to be with him so that I didn't have to feel this way. Another part of me hated him for making me feel so dependent on him. I was miserable again.

For the first time in my life, I was home alone. All by myself in a one bedroom apartment. Just me and my thoughts. It was unbearable. I couldn't stand the silence. There was so much noise around me back in Argentina and even all day while I was working in the office that I just didn't know how to do complete silence. When all was still, the noise in my head was deafening. I couldn't escape a single thought, and I didn't like any of them. They were mostly about me not being good enough and my place in the world. I was a pathetic mess.

By this stage, our printing company had moved offices and was in the middle of the City. As the months passed on, I began to take more notice of someone else at our printing company. Sarah was busy doing her own thing, and we had slowly grown apart since we had moved locations. We were no longer right next to each other as we were at our previous office space. The senior designers worked in their individual offices towards the back. The rest of us were all working at our desks in an open floor plan, but dividers separated us. My desk was directly opposite Daniel's office, and I was right at the back of the workstation now.

Sarah spent most of her time working with her office door closed. She shut me out of her life because she felt that being the only female senior, she needed to work harder than the rest. She had to prove herself and earn her place. As a result, I felt isolated from my co-workers. I missed my old friend. The girl that always had time to help me. The girl that had all the patience in the world for me. I no longer needed her help, but still loved talking to her and sharing our stories. My heart was full of gratitude for her.

My issue with being so close to Daniel was that I found him physically attractive. He was tall, thin, and had blond hair. His blue eyes were bluer than the sky itself, and his smile could melt the hardest heart. These were enough to make you fall in love. He was what I had dreamed about my entire adolescence. In addition to how gorgeous he was, Daniel was also kind and generous. He was a senior with a private office of his own, but he was never too busy to talk to you if you needed anything. Speak of temptation. I mean, if this was the Devil's work to steal my soul, He could have it right now, game over. You win, I'm not talking to God anyway, so who cares, right?

There was no need to worry, though. Daniel had been with his partner for sixteen years, and I had been with George for almost ten years now. So we were both in the same boat when it came to being in long term relationships with our partners. I hadn't told anyone at work that I was engaged to George. I didn't think it was the right time to tell anyone yet. That felt like a private thing to me. So, I figured I was safe. I didn't wear my ring because I just didn't like it. It was too bulky on my finger.

One evening, we had arranged to meet up with one of our co-workers, Harry, at a local pub for drinks at 7 pm. This night out is another funny story. We arrived at the bar on time, but we couldn't see Harry because he was short and there were too many people in the pub. It was so crowded that they were spilling out onto the sidewalk. We spent about an hour looking for him, but couldn't find him.

So, we got to chatting. Just Daniel and I for the first time since I had been working at this company. We had been working together for a few years now, but never actually talked to each other. I guess because we thought the other was off limits and vice versa. Now, I've never been a big drinker, and this was my first year of trying it out, but as everyone else drank alcohol in the office and it seemed the grown-up thing to do, I was giving it a go. So it didn't take much before I was dizzy and the next thing I knew, we were kissing.

We left the pub and went to get some dinner. We visited the train station three times before we could say goodbye to each other that night. Even then, we didn't want to leave each other, but it was the last train for the evening. The last thing he said to me was: "Monday is going to be interesting." We had all weekend to think about what had happened, as this was a Friday night. I felt like this was all a dream. I had walked into another dimension.

The evening with Daniel was not real. It hadn't happened. I spent the weekend thinking that I had imagined the entire thing. It wasn't until I walked in on Monday morning that I realized what he had said. It hit home. He smiled at me, and I knew that it had happened. It was real! What had I done? I was engaged, and Daniel had been with his partner for many years. So I convinced myself that these things happen when your loved ones are far away, and you feel lonely. I made a mistake. We just kissed, a lot, but it was no big deal.

George could easily forgive me for this minor slip. At the end of the day, true love conquers all, doesn't it? I would forgive him if he made this mistake. After all, we were far apart and missed each other terribly. At this point, I couldn't wait for this to be over and for George to finally be here with me. Being with George and making a life together was what I was concentrating on at the time. Once we moved in together, this would all be a distant memory. Little did I know what was in store for me.

I had to fight with the thoughts in my head. After all, I was engaged, and I had been with George for ten years now. What I was doing was adultery, even if my partner is a thousand miles across the ocean. I felt so guilty that I had not remained faithful to him. How could I be so weak? He was the man I was supposed to marry. We were going to have children and grow old together. George was my high school sweetheart.

Daniel and I spent the next few months getting to know each other more, and we knew that we wanted to be together. He was nine years older than me so I was certain the age difference would be a problem eventually. I told him I was engaged hoping that it would deter him, but it was meant to be, and George wasn't.

Looking back now, I realize that I had outgrown my relationship with George. Staying with George, no longer served my personal growth. I had learned everything I needed to learn about myself through him, and it was time to move on to a different experience. I always remember our time together with much gratitude and love. The moments I let go and just loved him and let him love me are beautiful memories that I will carry with me forever. For a very long time, I believed that my relationship with George was a waste of time. I lost ten years on this person. He was a mistake, and I couldn't get my time back.

But now as I look back on those ten years, I understand how worthy I was of his love. How deserving I was and that I was good enough because my heart was full of love for him and that was all that mattered. I write this as an example to you because I hear so many people talk about their past "mistakes" and I want you to know that there is no such thing. It is all for you. Every moment is there to show you who you are in every moment of your life. As long as you keep believing something about yourself, people and events will keep popping up to remind you that this is who you are now, at this moment. So I always give thanks for my first relationship because it led me to my second relationship.

So I spent ten full years afraid that I would lose him and finally did. Losing George created such relief because the incessant worrying didn't exist anymore. As I had lived by myself for a few years now, living on my own was a breeze. I wasn't afraid of being by myself anymore and no longer cared if nobody wanted me, because my freedom was more important now. I felt strong and confident again. Once you know you can manage on your own, you never want to feel that way again. That feeling that your happiness is in another person's hands.

But now something else had emerged in these years on my own. I no longer wanted to compromise and no longer wanted to put someone else first. It felt like everything I had learned in my life didn't work. It was never my job to change anyone else. My love cannot "fix" another person, and I would **never, ever, ever** again say that I am not good enough to be with someone. I went the other way and tried out being too good for someone.

I had given up life with a doctor. An incredibly smart man that could more than provide for both of us, so I had no qualms about walking out on anyone else that made me feel that they were better than me in any way, shape or form and I made sure I reminded Daniel of this every chance I got. It wasn't nice, but again, you learn what you are, after practicing what you are not. I practiced for ten years being unworthy of someone else's love; now I would practice being too good for anyone's love and see how that fits. There was no way I was going to make the same "mistakes" again. I was getting ready to make all new ones!

We moved in with Daniel's Mom, Emily, temporarily, while we looked for a place to live. Daniel didn't like where I was living at the time. I used to live in a rough neighborhood, and he had grown up close to the coast. It is much nicer out that way. I had grown up in these rough areas, so I didn't know any different. I thought all of Australia was the same. Straight away, I knew that Emily and I were kindred spirits. We had so much in common. It was so easy to talk to her. Again, I wished she had been my mom when I was growing up.

It would take me years before I could let go of the guilt and remorse I felt, for breaking George's heart. It didn't matter how many times I told him I was sorry; it never appeared to be good enough, and I just couldn't seem to move forward. Always thinking that what I had done was unforgivable and nobody could convince me otherwise. Hurting George could have been one of the reasons I was so awful to Daniel. Reminding him every chance I had that I had broken up with a dedicated, honest doctor just to be with him. Telling him that I had lowered my standards.

Also letting Daniel know continually, that I wasn't afraid to live on my own and wasn't prepared to put up with his crap, and I certainly wasn't going to waste another ten years with someone that wasn't worth it. I tried everything in my power to push him away. It's hard going into a second relationship when you take all the baggage from your first relationship with you.

I never thought this relationship would last. I honestly thought in the beginning, that we needed each other to terminate our previous relationships that no longer served either of us, but that it was just a means to an end. A stepping stone. It's hard to commit to a relationship when you haven't quite decided that the first relationship is over yet.

I mean, was that it? All the love I had poured into that individual signified absolutely nothing. He was not the love of my life as I had expected him to be. He was not my knight in shining armor here to rescue me from feeling unwanted and unloved. I started to question all those fairy tale stories you read as a kid. Was there any truth in any of them? I felt like I had believed a lie my whole life. None of it was real.

Here I was now, starting over again at almost thirty years of age. This period of my life was a very scary time for me. It was a time of uncertainty. My whole world had come crumbling down. George was the one thing I was absolutely, positively sure of and he was gone. This time in my life was full of doubt. I felt that there were so many questions and so little answers. My parents had given me so few skills for this thing called life.

As a result, I began to do a lot of reading. I needed to know the truth. Who was I? What was my purpose? Surely I could find the answers somewhere within the pages of people's lives who had struggled and survived. Not people with the same experiences as me, but rather, individuals who had overcome great adversity. Human beings that had been through much worse than me and had been able to find peace. People like Louise Hay, Wayne Dyer, and Neale Donald Walsch.

I read dozens of books, but nothing was bringing me closer to the truth. Why wasn't I blissfully happy? What was love? Real love, you know, the kind that makes you glow all over with joy and peace. While I was open to learning new ways of thinking, it was tough letting go of my old beliefs. After all, it had taken me a whole lifetime to decide all these things about myself and the world around me. It was foolish of me to expect that I would read a few books and all my problems would just vanish.

Sofia and I were reading the same books and constantly talking about what we had learned. We spoke to each other every single day, and we were always looking for answers. I was grateful to have someone to talk to about all these new ideas. All the things we never learned in our childhood that were so important. We didn't learn all these life-changing concepts because of our parents and their experiences. They didn't have all this knowledge to pass on to us. So it was up to us individually, to master it and make sure that one day it would be passed on to the following generation.

Understand that all of us are doing the best we can. With the information acquired in this book about who you are and why you did certain things in the past, better choices can be made. Every single day we continue to grow and learn more about ourselves.

With this new knowledge, you can improve even more. Don't beat yourself up for the mistakes you have made. Make an effort to learn from these errors so that you can be a better person and ensure not to repeat them again.

Nothing can change if we don't understand why we behaved a certain way. Change can only come as a result of you knowing who you are. Knowing who you were by studying your history. What made you the way you are today?

Because here lies the answer. Once you can understand **your** behavior, you will be able to understand others as well. Hence you will be able to see that we are all a product of our experiences.

What mistakes have you made in your past?

Can you rectify this deed? Can you say sorry and set things right? Apologizing will help you have closure and stop feeling guilty or sad.

Do you feel remorse about anything you have done in your past?

What have you learned about yourself from this experience?

Everything is there for you to discover more about yourself.

Chapter 6

WHAT'S HOLDING YOU BACK?

After a few months of living with Emily, Daniel and I moved in together to a gorgeous two bedroom apartment in a beautiful, green, leafy suburb near the City. It was fifteen minutes away from where we both worked, which was great. This was also a funny story. We had spent months looking for an apartment that was not more than thirty minutes away from the City, but they were out of our price range.

I thought we would end up paying for a very expensive apartment, just to be closer to work. We decided that for that price we should look for something closer to our printing company even if it meant paying a bit more, at least we would pay less for the train fare. When we saw this apartment, we couldn't believe it. We thought there had to be something wrong with it. It had no garage, but then we didn't have a car. It had a communal laundry and clothes line, but it had two bedrooms, a large bathroom and a kitchen with enough space to fit in a washing machine.

We were thrilled because it was exactly within our price range and so much closer to work and it was perfect. Our new home was in an exquisite suburb. We lived directly opposite a park. Life was good for a while, at least for one year. Five-minute walk to the train station and less than ten minutes on the train to get to work. Perfect! The living room space was quite large, and it had a small dining area. For the two of us, this apartment was more than enough.

What was different about this relationship was that we were clearly two separate beings. We didn't belong to each other. Daniel did not complete me. I no longer had to worry about pleasing him or what he needed because I was no longer afraid of being on my own. I knew that I could do that. Sex was a different experience as well. He was interested in pleasing me and making sure that I got enjoyment out of it. There are men out there that care about their partners having fun during sex. This concept was entirely new to me because I thought they were all the same in that department.

I had been jealous, clingy, needy and desperate in my first relationship. Putting all of George's needs and dreams before mine and in the process had become more invisible than I had ever been. I realized that I had to do something different if I wanted it to work. All of the things I had done before had eroded the relationship and forced it to end. These concepts were not a good foundation for a healthy relationship.

This time I would be my own person, with my own dreams and my own needs. This time I would accept him as he is. It is not my job to fix him or make him better. I can only change myself, and everyone else has the power to do the same. It was crystal clear to me that it was not my job to change him. After a couple of months of living together, we hired a piano. I couldn't believe it when I discovered that Daniel loved playing piano as well. He didn't know how to read music but could compose beautiful pieces from scratch.

Around this time, I felt that I needed answers. It was at this point that I started reading "Conversations with God" by Neale Donald Walsch. These books blew my mind. I wasn't ready to let God in yet, and I still had so much to learn about myself, that the information from these books would take at least twenty years to sink in.

I believe that everything I have been through has led me to understand all this information so much more. One thing is to have the knowledge in writing and words; another is to know it from experience. These books were the first step to freeing my soul of all the guilt it had been carrying for many, many years.

Another pattern would emerge around this time. That was my love affair with debt. I never learned how to manage money. My parents had a woeful relationship with money. They had left Argentina to have a better future because they had grown up in such poverty. Deep down, though, they felt that they didn't deserve abundance.

Just as an example, my mom had bought that beautiful china with the red roses. It was very expensive at the time. We never used it. We were always waiting for a special occasion, but the truth is that my mom didn't feel good enough to eat off these beautiful plates. She did this with many things. She bought beautiful, expensive handbags, or clothes or quilt sets, it didn't matter what it was, but they sat in her wardrobe for years without being used. My Mom loved buying these lovely things, but never felt worthy of having them. She never felt good enough to enjoy them.

I grew up hearing the words "there is no money for that," "we can't afford that," "that's too expensive" and "only corrupt people have money." My parents never had a savings account, only maxed out credit cards. They had lived a whole childhood unable to purchase fine things, so they weren't willing to wait to have them now.

Recently, thoughts of owning a stunning house plagued my mind. Thinking that then I'll be happy, and be able to feel comfortable having family and friends over to visit. Then I remembered that the first house my parents bought was tiny. It took my Dad many years to renovate it and fully brick the outside to make it look spectacular. We left for Argentina only a few short years after that.

In the end, we had two bathrooms, a rumpus room for my piano, and a huge kitchen with storage space to spare. It was unbelievable, but it was not enough to make us all happy. So I know in my heart, that having a magnificent house isn't the answer if deep inside yourself you feel that you don't deserve to have one. As long as you feel unworthy and undeserving of beautiful things you will just keep finding ways to reject them.

The other problem was that my parents had come from such poor backgrounds. As soon as they started working here and making some money, the banks offered them the credit card. Actually, in those days it was called the bank card. They could have everything instantly and pay for it later. Brilliant! They didn't realize that you end up paying twice as much for the same item because of all the interest you have to pay back.

That's what I witnessed as a child. So of course, as soon as I started working it was only natural that I sign up for a credit card and follow my parents' example. I didn't know any different and I didn't question it either. My parents never shared their issues with credit cards and debt, so I assumed that it was not a problem. They were of the mind that money is an adult subject and had nothing to do with children. It was looked upon as something dirty just like sex, so it was not discussed openly in front of us.

Back to the relationship. I was sure this relationship wasn't going to last because we felt so separate from each other. We didn't hold hands in public or hug or show much affection at all. For the first few years, Daniel would be checking out other girls as if he was still looking and still available. Almost, like he hadn't quite found the right one yet.

We lived together and had a great time together when we were on our own. I didn't commit too seriously because I had given my first relationship everything and I didn't feel ready to go all in. Maybe it was this lack of commitment, which made Daniel feel that he should keep looking elsewhere, as the partner he was with wasn't giving 100 percent to being with him. It doesn't help matters much either, if the person you are with, is always making you feel inferior and is always threatening to leave you.

I would have been looking for another partner too. Though somehow, I knew that what I was looking for, was not out there. What I was looking for did not come from another person, no matter how many other partners I had. I was so sure that the first relationship I had was true love. It felt like the real deal when I was in the relationship. That he was the love of my life and that we would be together forever. But none of that was true.

My Mom had already found all that in my dad. She couldn't have someone adore her more than my Dad does, and yet, it didn't seem to be enough for her. She didn't appear to be blissfully happy. He couldn't make her feel better about who she was.

I felt at this stage in my life that I needed to find myself again. Find out what I liked, what I needed and what I wanted. This time I wanted to read again to learn about life. In Argentina, I was too busy reading piano music in my spare time. There was enough reading to do with high school, with University, and for exams. But now, I needed to read books that would teach me about me. My priority now was to understand myself and others better. From this point in my life, I would devour book after book looking for answers.

I will be eternally grateful for my time with Daniel. For the first time in my life, he taught me just to say what I want to say. Whether I was angry or sad, annoyed or frustrated, Daniel always managed to show me how to let it out. I am also truly grateful for his mom Emily because she taught me that it is okay to be mad. It's okay to feel sad. She taught me to embrace all feelings. Every feeling you have is a gift to you.

As a child, I learned that it was bad to be anything but happy. If you weren't happy, there was something wrong with you. In truth, joy cannot be experienced without sadness, just as light cannot exist without darkness. Growing up, whenever my sister or I were upset or expressed any emotion that wasn't joy, my parents always pulled out the "when we were growing up" card. Their stories were awful, and it just made us feel guilty.

In retrospect, I'm sure they were trying to teach us gratitude. My folks were trying to show us how lucky we were to have two loving parents with a lovely home and everything we could ever need to be happy.

Both of my parents feel unworthy of love and undeserving of beautiful things, so they don't know how to just ask for what they want. They expect that whatever they do or give to someone that this person will reciprocate when it is their turn. Not having their favors returned has been a source of a lot of heartache and pain for my Mom and Dad. My Mom's pain goes so deep that it hurts when others touch her with love.

With Emily and Daniel, I learned to say *no* for the first time in my life. If I didn't want to do something, or if I didn't want something, I could say *no,* and it was alright. I was still loved, and the world did not come to an end because I said *no*. The more I said it, the less I felt guilty and became more comfortable with using this fabulous word.

It makes perfect sense to me now. When you say yes, but you don't want to do something for someone, you do it with negative energy. You do it with anger or frustration or annoyance. It feels more like an obligation, a chore. There is no love in what you are doing, and you are giving off a crappy energy.

When you say yes, and you want to do something for another person, your love will radiate through your actions. This energy spills over to others. You are giving them your love. When you understand that we are all connected and that everything you do affects others because of the energy you give off, this will become more and more important to you.

As children, nobody sat down with my parents and asked them what they wanted or what they needed. Adults just told them what to do, and if they didn't do as instructed, these adults punished them. So I guess, it wouldn't come naturally to them to ask for anything. Grown-ups did not sit down and talk to children in those days. They didn't think that youngsters had anything valuable to contribute to them.

Do you feel obligated to say yes, because you feel that others won't like you if you say no? I can promise you that if someone walks out of your life just because you say no, you are better off without them. Your job is not to please everyone that comes into your life and eventually you will learn that you won't be able to please absolutely everyone. Some people will never be happy no matter how hard you try. It is just their journey. There is something inside of them that they are yet to heal, so until they do, there's not much you can do for them.

You cannot go into someone's head and change the thoughts that are causing them mental suffering. Doing this for yourself is hard enough. As you push through your pain and the thoughts that cause you this pain, you will be able to see it in everyone you meet. We are all going through the same. Whether we had the simplest start or the harshest childhood, all of us are on the same journey. The journey to acceptance. Accepting ourselves for who we truly are.

Hollie Belle

Two of the hardest things I've learned in my life are the following:

1. Say what you mean to say. That way you don't have to resort to manipulation and making others feel guilty so that they'll do what you want them to do. Just ask for what you want.

2. Say *no*, when you don't want something, or you don't want to do something. Understand that as you have the right to say *no*, so do others. Saying *no* does not make you a bad person. We learn to put others first, and that makes us resentful because it does not come naturally to us.

What I've learned in recent years, is that debt is the same as being overweight or having an alcohol addiction, or any other kind of dependency. All of these things make us feel bad about ourselves, and they happen gradually over time. We slowly sabotage ourselves over many years. We buy things on credit with the notion that we can quickly pay it off. But here's the problem: you buy things because you believe that they will make you happy. At the very most the things I have bought have given me pleasure for a couple of months if that. Then you need something else to put in its place.

It's a vicious cycle that never ends. The more you buy, the more you get locked into debt, and soon, your cards are maxed out and need paying off before the banks lend you more. Then you are just paying off interest. You are stuck. Unable to buy that one more thing that will make you happy for the next couple of months.

I call these addictions, distractions because they distract us from the work that we need to do to move forward in our lives.

Pretty soon on my journey, something was going to happen that would magnify this problem.

I had left Argentina desperately longing for my freedom, my independence. Daniel was the same, so we respected each other's space. We hardly imparted any rules on each other. If I wanted my freedom to do as I please, I had to respect that he had the same right. But the universe was conspiring against me.

To be totally honest, I spent my 26th year infuriated with my mother. And my 27th and my 28th and my 29th and my 30th. I resented having to choose between my mom and George. Why couldn't I love both of them simultaneously? She tossed me aside when my sister was born, what did she care who I wanted to spend the rest of my life with anyway? I was furious with George because I had to end our relationship and this created great conflict within my mind. He refused to change, and I was fed up with having to choose between the two of them. It would take me several years before I could talk to my parents without any resentment.

While we were living so close to work, I learned to drive a car for the first time in my life. I learned to drive a manual car because then it's easy to drive almost anything. I took driving lessons for three months and got my P plates which meant I could drive on my own then. Learning to drive gave me such a sense of achievement. I felt that I could get the knack of anything after that. It seemed impossible in the beginning. I thought I wouldn't be able to do it and then did. It was an awesome feeling. It also gave me a real sense of independence. I could take myself anywhere and don't have to rely on anyone else. I loved driving.

Daniel and I had been living together for just over a year when Emily approached us with a proposal. The house she was renting was going up for sale, and the owner had offered it to her first before putting it on the market. He didn't need to sell it for another six months, so Emily invited us to come and live there with her and see if we liked the house enough to buy it with her.

As Emily was living on her own, the bank would not take the risk of lending her money for a house. This makes perfect sense. If she was injured and couldn't work, who would pay the mortgage? The proposal was that we would move in and if we didn't like it, that we would all buy a house together that we all liked and that suited the three of us. Emily had enough saved up for a deposit. Daniel and I had only just started getting into debt, so we had no money saved up at all. I believed that she was a free spirit, so I agreed wholeheartedly.

She had traveled all over the world following musical events. She was a huge Opera fan. Once we moved in, things changed, and it became evident that looking elsewhere was never the plan. She wanted to live in this house, and she didn't want to move. So Daniel and I had to make a decision together. I had only been with him for a little over one year, so this was a huge commitment for me. I could see that Daniel wanted to do this for his mom, so we all signed and bought the house.

One month after buying the house, Daniel and I went on a massive shopping spree. We bought furniture and kitchen appliances with no money upfront, but we knew we could pay it off. We felt we had no control over the decision of the house. Buying all this stuff was our way of feeling better about having to live in a house neither of us liked, and it made us feel that we had control over something.

We had gone from a two bedroom apartment overlooking the park to a one bedroom granny flat with a small bathroom and well, the kitchen was tiny too. We had to share the laundry downstairs, and we didn't have a garage we could use for our car. The driveway was too steep. Our backyard was full of huge rocks, and we had a puny piece of land with grass on it. We backed onto the National Reserve, so at least the view from the deck was breathtaking.

A couple of months later, we still didn't feel any better about living there. We painted the walls and painted the cupboards in the kitchen, but it was the same house. Nothing had changed. The suburb was very green and had lots of plants and trees, but every time I came down the street towards the house, I got this knot in my stomach. Yuck!

I was furious with Emily for the next few years because I felt manipulated into doing something and it made me feel that I was living with my mother all over again. If she had approached us and told us exactly what her intentions were, we probably would have said yes. It angered me that I felt deceived.

Please stay with me here. I am taking you through all of my moments: every single one of them. The pleasant and the unpleasant, that you may see how we create everything in our lives. Try to remember too, that this was about twenty years ago now.

The house we had moved into with Emily had two levels. Each level had its kitchen and its bathroom, which made it ideal for us all to live together. We made do, but it was difficult because neither of us liked the house. So it became uglier and uglier to us, and we would find more and more defects with it. I don't think it was the house that was the problem. If Daniel and I had bought it with the intention that we were helping out his mom, we both would have been happy with that decision.

We felt manipulated and deceived. Not a good way to start the next chapter of my life. At least, we were in this together. Lucky for us, we have always been honest and upfront with each other. It's nice to know I can count on him in that sense.

It's only saving grace was that the suburb was peaceful. I

felt that I had lost my freedom and my independence all over again.

Looking back now, I am full of gratitude for this moment in time. Emily was able to buy this house for herself, and the banks allowed Daniel and me to purchase the house we are living in today because we had partly paid off the first one. Without this moment, Daniel and I would still be renting. Emily was probably too embarrassed to come and ask us for help as she is so similar to me. Both of us feel that it's wrong to ask for help because we should be able to do everything ourselves. For me, this comes from being born here in Australia to immigrants who needed to work hard to get ahead.

The following year I began teaching piano, and to this day, it is something I love doing. You know when they ask you, what job would you enjoy doing even if you didn't get paid for it? Well, I'm one of those lucky people that get to do that. It was difficult getting started because none of the certificates I had from Argentina were acknowledged here in Australia. Fortunately for me, we could enroll students for piano exams whether we were certified or not.

So my journey of how to be the best music teacher began. The only problem I had, in the beginning, was that I didn't feel confident to charge the regular fees because the Australian Conservatorium of Music wouldn't acknowledge my previous studies from Argentina. Not being certified would be an ongoing issue for me. As I felt I wasn't worth much, I attracted people that treated me that way. Because Daniel and I were living in a one bedroom living space, I decided to teach in the students' homes rather than take up the afternoon with lessons in our home.

This way Daniel could do whatever he wanted at home and my work wouldn't be in the way. Also, our driveway, leading up to the front door was kind of scary. It was easy for students to slip and hurt themselves on the way in and out of lessons.

Some of the things I had to endure starting out, were parents that would cancel lessons and not pay for them. Other students would not be home when I came to lessons and didn't have the courtesy of letting me know they weren't going to be home. Some would cancel permanently at the last minute without any notice.

As I was doing this part time because I still had my full-time job at the printing company, I wasn't all that fussed at the time. It was when I had enough students to start working full afternoons and no longer needed my nine to five job that this would become an issue. All in all, the families I worked with were lovely people. I felt very blessed to have the opportunity to teach their children. In one of my families, even the dad signed up for lessons, and I taught him many years after his sons had finished learning with me.

The first two years in our new home were challenging, because of Daniel, Emily and I being heavy smokers. (At least a packet a day each). I was fed up with having to visit the doctor every three or four months with bronchitis, so was desperately trying to quit. I started smoking shortly after working at the printing company as everyone used to smoke inside in those days.

It's funny how things come back to you. I remember my doctor when I was five years old smoking in his room while he was examining me because I was sick. I remember my neighbors as I was growing up used to be heavy smokers, on both sides of the fence. Our friends used to mind Anna and me after school most afternoons, and they were smokers. My whole life I had been surrounded by smokers. It just didn't happen in my home. My Dad quit smoking when I was born.

It took me four years, but I finally gave it the boot. It's hard to quit an addictive habit when everyone around you is still doing it. I do believe that when you have had enough of something, you stop making excuses and just change it. I thought it was imperative to replace it with a healthy habit, so I started walking my dog twice a day. She was thrilled.

With the smoking, a problematic thought had been born. For this, I need to take you back to when I was growing up. My parents had become good friends with a couple from Italy. They had a little girl called Maria. She was younger than my sister, which meant that she would have been a toddler. These friends were chain smokers.

Every time we visited them, they would tell us that they had been in and out of the hospital with Maria because she had breathing problems. She had complications with her lungs. She always looked very pale and quite gaunt. I never forgot that little girl and always wondered if she would ever get to grow up or would she die before she became an adult. She used to cough a lot, and her nose was always stuffy and running.

I always left their house with a headache from the lack of oxygen. Smoking was quite fashionable in those days. The media wasn't bombarding us with the devastating effects it has on your health. Another event that would set this fear in concrete in my mind was our accountant at work when I was working at the printing company. She smoked all through her pregnancy and kept saying she wanted to quit but couldn't. Her little girl was also born with bronchial problems.

This fear of having a child with lung defects or bronchial problems would prevent me from having my child for over fifteen years! That's a long time to be afraid of something that hasn't even happened yet. I had been smoking for four years when I quit. Getting healthy became a top priority for me.

As Daniel continued to smoke, I still thought our chances of having a baby with health issues was quite high. I was not one of those people that enjoyed smoking. My smoking habit existed because everyone around me was smoking and I didn't see the point of being a passive smoker. I was constantly ill with bronchitis and visiting my local doctor for antibiotics. Deep down, I knew it wasn't good for my health, and I knew that I shouldn't be doing it.

Daniel was born into a house of heavy smokers. His mom smoked throughout her pregnancy and both his parents smoked throughout his childhood. So did both of my neighbors as I was growing up, and all of these children have grown up into adults without significant health issues. This was a normal way of life for them, but I didn't think about all the people I knew that had grown up without health problems. I remembered just one event in my childhood and kept my focus on that.

It was around this time that I had my first car accident. We spent the night at a 21st birthday party and the following day I woke up exhausted. I didn't want to go out this particular morning but felt obligated as my student was quite advanced and would need my help. I drove to her house anyway having had only two hours' sleep. We didn't have insurance on our car at the time. I ended up having to pay for our damages and the damages sustained to the other car as I took full responsibility for the accident. So now, our debt got that little bit bigger.

Anger and frustration are not good places to be. All they do is attract more things for you to be angry and frustrated. Our car was pretty old to start with, so we replaced it with a lemon we bought from a mechanic that lived at the end of our street. This time we bought insurance to cover any more accidents, which was just as well because this thing kept breaking down and always needed repairs and fixing.

More money wasted. The more I focused on our lack of money, the more we were drained of the little we had. Appliances would break down and would need replacing. Fines for speeding or traffic offenses came in abundance at this time. Bills were much higher than expected.

For example, the faucet would start leaking, and our water bill would be much larger than the previous one. A colder winter meant that the heaters needed to run for longer throughout the day leading to bigger electricity bills. And so on, and so forth. Just when you thought you got on top of it, you guessed it, the washing machine broke down and needed replacing.

Looking to improve our financial situation, I went to an interview with a music academy to offer my teaching skills. They offered me a job in the local schools giving music lessons. We had eight students per class. As the teacher, I had to take the eight keyboards with me to every school where I had to teach. Unpack them, give my lesson for forty-five minutes and then pack them back up again into my car.

I enjoyed this job immensely as it taught me so much but I found the quality of the lessons was unsatisfactory. Because we only taught once a week at each school, we had students of all different ages (from five to twelve years old), and the younger ones require more attention than the older students. Sometimes, the older students would end up with less than five minutes of my time all up. It didn't seem fair to them. The pay wasn't the best either because of course, the music school had to hire the hall at each school, and they had to pay for advertising. They had to provide the keyboards and batteries. In the end, there wasn't much left to pay the teachers. So, I only stayed at this job for one year.

In the middle of all this chaos, my sister came back to Australia. Anna wasn't having any luck finding a partner to share her life with in Argentina. So she decided to come to Australia and search here. I felt at the time that my sister wouldn't let me in. She had no interest in us being close or getting to know each other at all, and I guess that is only fair.

I had never even tried to get to know her, and when I was with George, he was always berating her and belittling her. I never once defended her or told him not to say nasty things to her. He was letting out his resentment for his parents' separation on her. I knew this, and yet, did nothing. She was only a teenager and at that time when you are forming your self-image. Your ideas about who you are. He would have had a massive influence on crushing her self-esteem.

I don't think that it helped, that when we were growing up, I remember my Mom always saying to her, "Why can't you be more like your sister? She never complains. She studies hard and gets good grades at school." My thoughts were always: "If I was so great, why did you toss me aside?" Still, being compared to someone else all the time, can't be good for your self-esteem.

I hear many parents do this. You are telling your child that they aren't good enough as they are when you say why they can't be more like someone else. The truth is that Anna is awesome at manual work. She loves making jewelry from scratch which is stunning. Anna is very creative with her hands. She learned to be a designer and is brilliant at sewing up children's clothes. She's also amazing in the kitchen, whereas I find cooking boring. But that doesn't make me a bad person or not good enough. Creating delicious dishes does not interest me in any way. I lose interest quickly and end up overcooking most of the meals I make. To date, I've burnt a pot just by boiling water in it to get some pasta cooked.

I completely forgot that I left it on the stove top. Next thing I know, I can smell a terrible odor coming from the kitchen. I've overcooked rice, pasta, eggs, and pancakes, well pretty much anything I try to cook. If it takes more than two minutes of my time, I'm out of there and lose all concept of time. It's just an example. You may be an outstanding chef. That is your gift.

Mine is music and learning. Not all of us are good at the same things.

And the truth is that we are not meant to be. Otherwise, we would all be doctors, or astronauts or composers. We'd all have the same profession. Then where would we be? We wouldn't have bakers or butchers or teachers. Carpenters, electricians, and veterinarians wouldn't exist. We need to be different. It is essential for our survival. It is also vital to your personal growth. You need others to challenge you with opposing views to your own.

I want you to think about yourself at this point.

Forget everyone else.

I want you to make a list of all your strengths.

Not only things you know how to do like cooking, teaching or gardening, but also things like being a good listener and caring for others.

Are you a patient person?

Are you kind?

Maybe you are good with animals.

It is easy to get caught up in all the things that we are not and ignore all the things that we are.

Think about your possessions.

Think about all your belongings.

Make a list of all the things that made you happy.

How long did this happiness last?

Why did you buy these items?

What were you going through at this time in your life?

How was this going to make your life better?

   Make a list of all the things you believed at this point. Anything that has held you back from having something you wanted. In my case, I thought that having a child while I was still smoking would mean that she would have health issues because of my addiction.

Chapter 7

WHY ARE YOU SO ANGRY?

So, here I am now, mid-thirties and still no child of my own. I love children and have always loved them from quite a young age. Being a child was such an enjoyable experience to me, that I assumed that all children had wonderful childhoods. I am working full time now as a piano teacher. Doing courses to learn more about music and different ways to teach in my spare time

When I turned thirty, I had a very vivid dream that would make me doubt things I had believed about myself. In my dream, I was pregnant and was at the hospital ready to give birth. When the baby comes out, I am looking at its little face and realize that the baby is me. The person holding me was my mom. I could feel everything she was feeling at the time. She did love me, and I was special because I was her first baby. I started to think about her in a different way.

At this point in my life, I signed up to do a music course that focused on teaching small children under the age of five. It is about learning music through movement and feeling it in your body. Here, I would learn to improvise music which I had never done before. There were just two of us signed up to complete this course. The other person was a girl called Sharon.

She was also a piano teacher, and we lived just a few suburbs away from each other (less than ten minutes away). We used to carpool to get to our fortnightly classes, which was over an hour away from both of us. Our course teacher Susan, was brilliant and we both gained so many useful skills, but Sharon was to be the best teacher I had ever had so far.

It was through our talks in the car on our trip to see Susan one day that I told Sharon about my Eisteddfod and what a traumatic experience this had been for me. I had never spoken to anyone about this incident. It completely opened up my eyes to what the doctor meant when he said that it was all in my head. The fear of recreating that event was so great in my mind that it created the disease so I wouldn't have to face that situation ever again. The fear paralyzed me, immobilizing me, preventing me from using my hands at all. Even for simple day to day tasks like washing my hair and brushing my teeth.

It was after this conversation with Sharon that I got to thinking and decided to seek the help of a hypnotherapist. My local doctor was a hypnotherapist, and I could see her for this service through my health care card. That way it didn't cost me anything. I started having sessions with her regarding this fear and my performance anxiety. It was more about affirmations and talking about what had happened. Learning how we could get over this fear so that I could move on. I felt stuck in my life and knew that this was deeply entrenched in my subconscious.

Halfway through my hypnotherapy sessions, I had another car accident. I didn't want to see my doctor that morning. It was raining, more like it was bucketing down, and I just didn't feel up to it but thought I should continue not wanting to lose my momentum. We were two weeks late with our payment for the car insurance, and yes, you guessed it, we had to pay for the damages out of our pocket. The insurance company wouldn't cover it, even though I was not at fault this time. The other car had lost control going around the roundabout and ran into me head on. I got the license plate number, but the police came back to tell us that it was a stolen vehicle. It had three young, teenage boys in it at the time.

Daniel and I were fed up with this car always breaking down. So we bought another second-hand car to replace it. Unfortunately, we also bought it through our neighbor from the end of our street, as he was a mechanic. Another lemon! What luck! But it was the last car we would purchase from this neighbor.

It was around this time that I finally decided to send George his ring back. He had been asking for years, but I figured that he wasn't in any hurry to marry me. What was the rush to marry anyone else? Yes, I was still furious at him. He didn't miraculously change into this man that loved me unconditionally and had no faults at all. I was angry that my love wasn't enough for him and that I wasn't good enough for him.

But I was the one that had decided right from the beginning that I was beneath him and didn't deserve him. So in truth, I created this outcome. My first relationship was based more on the fear of losing him than actually loving him. Therefore the chances of its survival were not favorable. Please let me state again here that he never said anything or did anything to make me feel inferior. He did love me and was kind and loyal.

The last thing he had said to me was that another man would only want me for sex and would never love me for who I am. They could never love me the way he did. In other words, no other man could ever love me. I was unlovable. How dare he say that to me? After all the love I wasted on him? Thousands of kisses and hugs, wasted. Thousands of smiles, thousands of "I love you" and thinking he was so exceptional, wasted, lost, gone forever. It was just a feeble attempt to make me change my mind.

I tried to move forward, yet again. One year after Anna arrived in Australia, Mom and Dad came to visit. Anna had come to Australia in search of her true love, and my parents were worried about her living out here on her own. She didn't want to live with us. Anna's visit taught me that we are all looking for own happiness, just as my parents had done previously.

My parents came all this way to a foreign country, to a place with an unknown culture, a language they didn't know how to speak, in search of a better life for all of us. Many of our relatives came to Australia with the same hopes and dreams. I think for many of them, their main hope was to leave their past behind them.

But from my experience, ignoring the past, trying to bury it and not think about what you have been through because it is too painful, keeps you stuck in certain patterns. True freedom to create something new can only come when we look at the events that have taken place in our lives, and we can see the gifts in them. When we can understand that each event has made us exactly who we are today, and be truly grateful for every moment that has brought us to this moment in time. They are all blessings, every single one of them.

As painful as the memory may be and as unacceptable as the behavior may have been of how someone treated you, understanding that this person was in tremendous pain themselves and they are just passing on all they have experienced, is your first step to freedom. Understanding that their behavior was never about you, but a reflection of the immense pain inside of them. A person with a heart full of love cannot harm another person. This person understands that we are all connected and that what hurts others, hurts us in return.

I decided to take piano lessons with Sharon. She had completed all the courses through the Conservatorium of Music, and she was a concert pianist. I found her lessons invaluable. Each teacher gave me different skills. My teacher in Argentina taught me all about rhythms, enough so, that I have never had a rhythm, I couldn't work out to this very day.

Elisa had taught me about technique, but her technical work required that the fingers lift high off the keys and strike down quite hard. Elisa also exposed me to so many wonderful composers. I was so grateful for my time with her. She was not only my teacher, but my friend, and I loved her dearly.

Sharon would teach me to keep my fingers always touching the keys. This method has made a huge difference to my playing and my confidence. She also taught me something else. Every time she would ask me to do something on the piano she would explain the logic behind it. I loved this method. It helped me to remember why I was doing certain things when I played and it made sense to me. It made it more real to me. I loved this method, so much so, that I still do this with my students today.

Six months after doing our course with Susan, Sharon and I flew to Queensland for a two-week course of intensive training to practice what we had been learning in her classes. It was during this trip that I met a young girl who was twenty-five years old. Hannah had also started learning piano at the age of ten, but her piano teacher didn't tell her that she was too old. As a result, she had completed all of her studies and was a concert pianist. Hannah wasn't interested in pursuing this as a career because she wanted to be a school principal. That's what brought her to this program we were all studying.

It got me thinking. Why didn't Hannah's teacher tell her that she was too old? It seemed unfair. What gave my piano teacher the right to say that to me? Who gave her permission to squash a little girl's dreams like that? This memory made me furious. I felt real hatred for that first piano teacher. It was her fault that I had given up on my dream of becoming a concert pianist. It was her fault that I spent years suffering when I lost my confidence because she had not taught me the right rhythm of that piece and made me embarrass myself in front of all those parents and students that day at the competition in the City.

Sharon and I were both homesick after just two days of being there. I missed Daniel terribly and my pets back at home. Up until this trip, I had taken it all for granted. We couldn't wait to get home. I had never been more than a few days apart from Daniel. Every six months he would travel for work at the printing company to talk to our clients in other states of Australia, but he was never away for more than ten days at a time. But that was years ago now.

At this point in our relationship, I approached Daniel about getting married. I knew we were both deliberately putting it off. We wanted to be together. That wasn't the issue. The thought of getting married was not a joyful one for us, mostly because Daniel's parents hated each other with a vengeance, even though they divorced each other twenty years ago. They could not be in the same room together. I was fortunate to have my parents and my sister here with me, but they weren't talking to any of our relatives here in Australia. And I couldn't have a wedding with just my parents and sister and not have any of my cousins.

You see this is what happens. How many of you out there, have been separated or divorced from a previous partner, and can't stand to be in the same room together? Twenty years is a long time to hate someone. But as long as you keep sweeping your past under the rug, that's where you will keep finding yourself. Never being able to release that moment in time. Never being able to move on. Always feeling uncomfortable even at the mere mention of their name.

So, we decided to elope. We booked a holiday for two weeks in Perth and got married there. Just the two of us. No family, no friends. Just us. A few years before our wedding, one of our work colleagues from the printing company had moved there, and we had contacted him to see if he would serve as our witness.

So Martin and his son agreed to be our witnesses for the day, and that was all we needed. The hairdresser styling my hair that morning said that she wasn't quite used to the bride being so calm. I felt at peace. We had a beautiful ceremony. A day that I shall treasure forever in my heart.

Sadly two days after we returned from Perth, Daniel's father passed away. He had been battling lung cancer for quite a few years. Unfortunately, even after being diagnosed with cancer, he never stopped smoking. He had given up on life at this point and wasn't interested in getting better or improving his chances of healing his body.

My first ten years with Daniel were very rocky. I was dealing with my guilt of breaking up with George, plus I was mad at pretty much everyone at this stage of my life. Angry with my parents because I blamed them for my first relationship failing. I felt that they had interfered and hadn't let me work things out for myself.

George spent his energy focusing on fighting with my parents and sister, instead of focusing on what was important: *loving me*. So this infuriated me as well. I felt that he left me no choice but to end it, due to his relentless vendetta against my parents. In truth, it felt like he was releasing all his anger from his parents onto mine. His dad cheated on his mom all those years, and George felt embarrassed and disgusted by his father's behavior. So he would take it out on my Mom and Dad because he couldn't tell his parents how he felt about their separation.

My heart was full of rage for Emily. Daniel and I never got to choose the house we wanted to live in. That's a pretty big decision to make even when you do all agree. Our cars kept breaking down, and we couldn't afford to buy a good car. The vehicles not functioning properly infuriated me to no end. I was angry with our neighbor because he sold us two crappy cars in a row. I was frustrated because no matter what I tried, I just couldn't make more money to get ahead. This was not the life I dreamed of having when I was growing up. I felt disheartened and annoyed with my life. Even Daniel irked me because he wouldn't quit smoking to help me make a healthy baby.

The day of our wedding, I felt a bond between us. A strong feeling that we were meant to be together. I was happy to bury my past with George and move on. I could talk to my parents again without feeling anger. They looked at me as an adult that could make wise decisions for herself. My parents finally trusted that I knew what was best for me. I am so grateful for this relationship because it has always been about our personal growth.

The day we married something changed inside of me. There was no need to be better than Daniel. I was happy to look at him as my equal. He deserved my love, and I deserved his. We have had a deeper connection since then. Up to that point, I was always threatening that if I wasn't satisfied with the relationship that I wasn't wasting my time. I wasn't afraid to walk out the door and live on my own, rather than have to put up with someone else's crap.

The peaceful feeling that swept over me meant that there was no need to run away anymore. For the first time in a long time, I felt safe and was where I needed to be. I wish I could say that we lived happily ever after, but I buried my past. Occasionally my past would come back and bite me in the butt because I did not make peace with it or resolve any of my issues in any way.

You see, I understand now that people come into your life

to help you grow. They challenge you in ways that you may not have ever seen for yourself because they are looking at the world in a different way to the way you are viewing it. The sum of their experiences has shaped them into who they are, just as it has molded you into who you are.

Six months after our wedding, we approached the bank, and they granted us a loan for a second mortgage. Now Daniel and I could have our home. Finally, we had our place now. I was still pretty angry with Emily at this point, and this would take many years to get over.

Now, this is an ongoing pattern that I will address in later chapters. Why was I angry all the time? Where did this anger originate? I couldn't enjoy my life while these thoughts of rage kept consuming me. Had this feeling always existed? If so, it must have started at some point in my life. I wasn't born angry. Was I? But then, when did it start and why?

As hard as it has been to change, I would learn ever so slowly, to speak up when I don't like something or something upsets me. Standing up for myself was difficult because it went against everything I had learned so far. The hardest thing for me to master was to say **no** when I don't want to do something or simply didn't want something. In the past, I had learned that this was selfish. So we did things in a huff because we felt obligated to say yes. Saying *no* meant risking that others might not like us anymore.

We had just moved in and were barely covering the mortgage repayments plus all the bills. My predominant thoughts were about losing the house we had just bought, which meant losing our freedom and independence again. I had to drive more than twenty minutes by car to get to my students. Some were even thirty minutes away. What if the vehicle broke down and I couldn't keep teaching? I couldn't sleep at night. I didn't want to go back to the life I had just left behind. The independence and the freedom to do whatever we wanted to do, was too important to Daniel and me.

All I could think about was the lack of money we had and how it wasn't enough. How will I pay the bills? How will I pay the mortgage? I don't want to lose the house! It stayed in that pattern for many, many years.

It was at about this time, that my neighbor that lived directly behind our house began complaining about my dog barking all the time. She was a little mini foxy cross called Milly, and she yapped a lot. We had only had her at our previous house for two years, and now we had only been in our new home for six months. She was eight years old when I picked her up because the owners were moving to an apartment and couldn't take her with them.

So this poor little dog, every time the front door would open she would go flying out and charging down the street. I am guessing that she was looking for her previous owners. They had two little girls that used to play with her and she must have missed them terribly. So she hadn't had much time to adapt to a new home with us yet. Milly had already been to two different houses with us.

Now an ongoing feud with this neighbor would commence and take years to resolve. I mean, they had a dog too. How could they be so heartless? How could they not understand that she was just getting used to her new home? To make matters worse, their three-year-old daughter enjoyed tapping on the fence with a stick to make Milly bark because she thought it was funny, as children do. I never said anything because I didn't believe that it was a problem until they came to complain. The only reason the matter resolved itself was that four years later, these neighbors sold their house and moved overseas.

Now here is where I would like to make a comment. People will come into your life to let you know what you are feeling and giving out to the world. It doesn't necessarily need to be the person you have been unkind to or the person you are harboring ill feelings for and this is where a lot of people get confused. My neighbor was just letting me know that I was not being loving towards others and was angry at too many people. If I kept up this attitude more things would come into my life to annoy me and frustrate me.

So my fear of losing my work due to my new location became a reality. My car broke down, and we couldn't afford to buy another one. Daniel was now working for a computer company and needed the car to get to his work. We had already taken out a loan for that car. I decided to start working from home. My fear of losing my job had become a reality. I only had four students that could come to me in my new home, therefore, having to start all over again.

I had to advertise locally and wait for the business to build up again. Now I would attract a whole new kind of student. The kind that doesn't show up for a lesson and doesn't pay you for it. Students that just drop out and don't have the courtesy to let you know that they aren't coming back. Parents that show up late all the time, but expected a full lesson anyway, even though, now other students would have to wait ten to fifteen minutes to have their turn. I didn't have the courage to say that I needed to finish their lesson on time because it's not fair to those who are punctual.

I wanted to include all of this for those of you who, just like me, don't feel worthy of standing up for yourself because you worry that these people that mistreat you will leave and talk trash to others about your business. For those of you who don't feel worthy of charging what you are worth. The years of me starting my business from scratch here in my new home were tough.

I must say here, that we attract these people into our

lives with what we are thinking and feeling consistently. My predominant thoughts were of anger and scarcity, so of course, I was receiving more to feel angry and frustrated with, and money was not flowing smoothly.

I used to visit Mom and Dad once a week in Adelaide, where my sister lived now. On my way there, I would stop off at a nursing home that was five minutes away from them, and I would play the piano there for free for an hour. I thought this would help me to build up my confidence with my performance issues. It was nice having Mom and Dad here and not feel angry with them anymore. My anger had diverted to Emily and to my neighbor, who I thought was very inconsiderate in regards to my dog.

Let's get back to my relationship with Daniel. In between all the music courses, I studied from books and the internet how to get pregnant naturally. I guess that the classes and the finance problems kept me distracted from the fact that I hadn't fallen pregnant yet, not even once. As the years passed on, it became harder to get through Christmas and New Year's Eve, because each year I would have but one wish: Please universe, let it be my turn this year to have my little girl. We had picked out the name Abigail for over eight years. We were starting to think that this name was jinxed. So each year after that, every New Year's Eve, we picked out a new name for our little girl.

In the months to follow, my sister found an American on the internet that lived in Florida. Initially, they fell in love in a chat room where single people meet. After that, they would speak over the phone for hours. He sent her tickets to go and visit him in America, and he came to see her here in Australia. She finally looked happy. We were a bit apprehensive. I mean, we didn't know anything about him. When Anna went to see him in Miami, my Dad was saying, "Should we be worried?" He could be a serial killer stalking women on the internet for all we know. Lucky for us, he wasn't.

At this time in my life, one of my cousins in Argentina passed away. She had been struggling with Leukaemia for years and finally gave up. I had spent many weekends playing with this cousin when I lived there, and this disturbed me. It made me reassess my life. I hadn't achieved anything yet. I hadn't accomplished anything. My life had no meaning.

Her death also made something else very real for me. We don't know when it is our time to die. I never cried when she died. Maybe it was because it didn't seem real to me as I wasn't there to witness her passing. Somehow deep inside, I knew that one day we would see each other again and what for us seems like years and decades, to her, would be a blink of the eye. I knew this because when I had been distressed about George's grandfather passing away, he came to visit me and he was happy. So I knew she was okay and that I would see her again when it was my time.

It was during these years that a disgusting habit would form. As nobody had ever taught me how to handle money, and I never even looked into it myself, I would spend more than what we were bringing in. Not realizing at the time that I had a problem with money, I was always behind with the mortgage payments. Always focusing on losing the house because I couldn't keep up with the payments, started creating a particular pattern in my life.

Every few months when it got too much I would approach Emily and ask her to borrow the money for the mortgage. The problem was that I would sabotage myself and somehow never have the money to give back to her. Despite this, she never said *no* to me. Like, I say many times in my book, she treated me like her daughter. Borrowing from Emily made me feel awful, especially when I had to keep going back to ask her again and again. She could see that I was conflicted but just wanted to help.

I understand now about addictions. You do things, believing in that moment, that it will feel great, but then it doesn't take long before you feel lousy about yourself. This quick fix, happens with drugs, with binge eating, with alcohol. We use these tools to feel better temporarily, but in the long run, they make us feel terrible. Debt is no different. We accumulate debt until no more can be added to the pile then we are stuck having to pay it off. Losing sleep because we can't pay our bills on time or at all in some cases.

I was in the habit of buying things to make me feel happy, but then the money would run out, and I felt helpless and useless that I wasn't good enough to provide for myself. What is the point of working if you can't buy the things you want to have, right? I might as well be on welfare and live day by day just surviving because this was not living. I knew deep down inside of me that there is an abundance. There is more than enough in the universe for all of us.

What I didn't know was that I wasn't letting it in because of my feelings of unworthiness. Not being worthy of having it. So I kept pushing it away. It was a real love-hate relationship. I love you because of all the magnificent things you allow me to buy, but then hate you because of the remorse that eats away at my soul. It's a no-win situation.

My parents and the Church taught me from such a young age, that money is evil. It is not good to have money because only corrupt people are wealthy. Not only that but as children, we weren't even allowed to talk about money. It was a subject that only adults discussed and even then, it was a negative topic. So I felt guilty if I made too much money from my lessons.

My Dad made an excellent living as a bricklayer. As he perfected his craft, he was able to become self-employed. My parents could have been very well off, but they didn't know how to manage their income. They didn't know how to save money. As they both grew up in poverty, this was a new concept to them. Neither of them had any idea what credit was until they got to Australia. Tax time was a time of year that my parents dreaded because they had to pay out more money and they didn't put any aside to be ahead for when it came around.

I know how they felt because as an adult, this is what I have done. As a piano teacher, I work for myself and the same thing would happen every single year when it was time to lodge my taxes. I cringed every time I had to put together all my paperwork in preparation for taxes. Not once did I think to put some cash aside every month so that the money would be there when it was time to pay. Instead, I'd spend nights in a panic that I didn't have the money to pay that bill.

It is nuts really. Not having to pay tax, made me ecstatic, but this meant that I hadn't earned enough money to get over the threshold that requires payment, which indicates that I was making less than $20,000 a year. The more tax I had to pay, the more money was made overall in that year. Therefore, shouldn't I be excited to be paying more tax instead of less? Like I said, **nuts**!

But this has been the same for everything. I was never grateful to pay my bills. Instead of being happy to pay for the electricity that keeps my house warm in winter and cool in summer. This utility lights up my house at night time and gives me so much comfort and remarkable things to enjoy like television and my computer. **Nope!** I was annoyed that I had to pay it. My phone that allows me to speak to my family and friends. The water bill that allows me to keep everything clean including myself.

All I remember growing up was mom complaining about how expensive all the bills were and how she dreaded going to the mailbox because that's where the bills came in those days. Nowadays, we get to shudder every time we go to our mailbox and every time we open up our emails. Twice the fun! We resent our money going out. Is it that we don't trust it will come back to us? Do we not have faith that we can make more to cover all the expenses? We are always focusing on not having enough.

Now this baffles me. We never went without electricity or a roof over our heads when I was growing up. We always had a phone that worked. I had more than enough clothes to wear for all the different seasons and various pairs of shoes for different occasions. Food to eat and water to drink were always abundant in my home. So, where did these thoughts of lack come from in my mind?

I believe that it was inherently passed on by my parents. They did go without food and sometimes didn't have enough to wear to keep them warm in winter. So, they knew what it was to be cold and hungry. Both of them had to start working at a very young age to help provide for their households.

As a result, neither of them wanted us to endure the same hardships. They didn't want us to know what hunger was or what it felt like to be cold because you don't have warm clothes or shoes to wear. Also, they didn't want us to work before we finished high school because education was the most important thing to them. They believed that knowledge is power and gives you the tools to succeed in life. They wanted us to have all the opportunities that they never had as children.

That was the main reason that they came to Australia in the first place. As much as it was so easy for them to have everything they could want here, it wasn't enough to erase all those childhood memories filled with scarcity Every chance Mom got, she told us how lucky we were and how rough they had both had it as kids. Funny enough, though, she seemed to think that Dad's childhood was harder than hers. Imagine that! Mom had lost both of her parents at the age of five.

I guess it must be difficult having both of your parents and feeling that they don't love you. Dad's mom didn't show any affection. We know because she didn't display any affection for any of her grandchildren either. Being a grandparent is where parents usually shine. Giving their love to their grandkids, where they don't have the responsibilities the parent has. Then again, it must be difficult watching your husband beat your children to a pulp and not be able to say anything. Her job was to cook and clean and just have kids. She had no say.

She never interfered with the way our grandfather disciplined his children. My Dad never saw his mom stand up for him or any of his siblings. Our grandmother accepted that this was the way it needed to be done. Her childhood must have been the same, so it was not unusual for her.

I encourage you to look at the people in your life today.

Make a list of all the people you are angry with, or that have annoyed or offended you.

Write down the reason you are upset with each person.

Look carefully at your list. Is it about you being right and that person being wrong?

Look carefully at your reasons. Are there things you believe about yourself that do not serve you, (things that make you feel bad).

Example: I am angry with my mom because she still treats me like a child and keeps telling me what to do. She doesn't respect me as an adult and does not trust that I can take care of myself.

*You know, after being a parent for so many years and telling you what to do, it is hard for them to know when to let go and accept your choices. Sometimes, they just want to know that their opinion is important. They need to know that what they have to say matters and that **they** matter. It is hard for them not to feel needed and wanted anymore, like when you were little.*

So you see, it was never about you. It is always about how others are feeling and how they see themselves. Be kind. If that person didn't care, they wouldn't try at all.

Do you feel that you can't take care of yourself? Do you think that you can't make the right choices for yourself?

Look at your list very carefully. Go through and write down all the good things these people have done for you because I can promise you that they may have done one thing that upset you, but they have done hundreds of things to show you that they love you.

Chapter 8

MAKING AMENDS

This chapter is unbelievable. So much can happen in just five years! First on the list would be that my sister got married to her gorgeous American man. They had a lovely wedding in the City. I remember feeling distressed that day with my life. I cried at the reception thinking that my relationship with Daniel was surely over.

We couldn't have a baby, and we were growing apart. I went to see a naturopath in the hope that she could help, but I was on my own. Daniel doesn't believe in natural remedies, and I guess he probably just figured that it wasn't meant to be after ten years of trying. I had been keeping charts, recording my temperature every month to see when I ovulated. Buying kits off the internet. Trying anything and everything to fall pregnant.

Daniel was still smoking, and he loves his alcohol too, but that's a cultural thing here in Australia. I felt that he wasn't doing anything to improve our chances of falling pregnant. I asked him so many times to please just quit temporarily to give us a better chance, but Daniel was adamant that it wasn't him. In my eyes, he was selfish and insensitive. It filled me with rage that he wasn't even trying because even if he didn't care about becoming a parent himself, it had always been my dream to be a mother. To know what it is to carry your child and feel it grow inside of you.

Shortly after their wedding, my sister and her husband moved to Florida, mainly because this is where he had his work. He was a lawyer in a very prestigious firm and well respected in the town where he resided. My sister could easily take her job with her where ever she lived.

Soon after Anna's wedding, I went for a job interview with a music school near my home. They paid for me to do a one-week training course in Queensland. I loved this week away. It meant that I could teach music in the mornings and would finally be making more money. I would get to sing for all these lessons, and that was something that filled me with joy. I came back to Adelaide, and we had the second week of full training for their classes here where the school was.

Once I finished the training, they offered me Monday mornings, and that was it! I couldn't believe it! Why would you pay to send someone off to Queensland and then pay for a whole week of training here in Adelaide to offer them just one morning of work? Teaching the younger courses meant not practicing any of the courses I had learned in the second week of training. Are you kidding me? One morning of work was not enough. It was barely two hours' worth of work.

I asked them what afternoons I could do, and they only had Mondays available, but they desperately needed someone for Saturday mornings. I took Monday evenings for one term, but was losing money. They were paying me less than half of what I was making at home. Plus I had to travel there by train to teach. At home, the students came to me, so there was no time wasted on commuting to get to them. Saturdays were the same. I gave up some of my students to work for this new school, and the pay was less than half again.

When was I ever going to make some real money? Every

time I tried something new, it failed. I was under contract, as they make you sign one before you start your training. My contract with the school expired after two years. Fortunately, this music school decided to change over to a new system at the end of my first year. They were purchasing a different franchise, which meant that I had to redo all my training if I wanted to stay with them. I politely declined.

I thought that the year I had spent at this school was not worth it. What was the point of that? They only offered me one morning per week. How was that supposed to help me financially? I ended up making less money as I cut my private classes to take on their classes. It never occurred to me to ask, but the training in itself was invaluable. I learned that repetition is the key when it comes to teaching. It seems like I had wasted my time, but as a result, I gained so much knowledge.

I never learned how to practice with any of my previous teachers. This school taught me to chunk it down. Cut the piece into smaller parts and repeat within these shorter sections. Depending on the difficulty, you can learn each hand on its own. I had always played the piece straight through a million times, and this was not effective. I found that a piece of music would take me five times longer to learn. Not only that, but learning it in bite-sized bits, helps you to memorize it so much easier. So again, what I thought was a total waste of time, was an amazing experience that added to my teaching and playing skills.

I also experienced firsthand, specific methods designed for infants in this system that help you teach music and rhythm without an instrument. This knowledge in itself was invaluable. Nothing that you do is ever wasted. It is all there ideally placed just for you and your growth.

After this, I decided to look into doing something different. So I completed a gym course and found work at a fitness center close to home for about four months, but realized that it was also draining when it came to money. You see to continue to teach as a gym instructor; you need to attend specific courses to improve your skills. These courses were all very expensive. You need to complete a certain amount of points in their system to continue working as a gym instructor. Otherwise, you lose your license to work in the fitness industry.

With music, the courses I had completed were because I wanted to know more. They were not compulsory. The job at the gym was less than half what I was making at home, and it was hard work. You had to earn it. The good thing about it was that I was the fittest I had ever been. I felt healthy and full of energy, and was fortunate to learn all about nutrition, which is vital for our survival.

So my love-hate relationship with money continued. It seemed that every time I spent money on a course in the hope it would increase my income, it would put me further in debt and further away from my dream of becoming financially independent and wealthy. The gym course cost me $5,000, and that went on the credit card.

I went back to teaching and decided to set special rates for adults throughout the mornings. With a bit of luck, some adults started taking lessons with me plus a couple of retired folks. Teaching adults was a joy, because you don't have the pressure of sitting exams with them. They just learn for their leisure, and it was nice to see them each week.

After turning forty, Daniel and I visited the IVF clinic for the first time in search of answers. The doctor asked me to have a laparoscopy to see if there was anything wrong with me that could be preventing us from falling pregnant. I felt devastated. They couldn't find any physical evidence as to why I had never fallen pregnant. There was nothing wrong with me.

I was sore for three days after the procedure and was very

sick from the anesthetic. Having to cancel all my lessons that afternoon. Why was I being singled out? There are women in the world who smoke throughout their pregnancies; they do drugs, they drink alcohol, and yet here I was walking every day, eating healthy and keeping fit to become a mother. It seemed incredibly unfair.

On our way back from my day surgery, Daniel sold our car so he could buy his first road bike. By this stage, I was working seven days a week. Yes, even Sundays because I figured I didn't work full days throughout the week. So I needed to work Sundays if we wanted to get ahead financially, especially now that we were getting into motorbikes as this is not a cheap hobby to have.

I decided that I wanted to learn to ride too. After all, why should Daniel be having all the fun, right? So, I signed up to do my L plate's course and passed that. I bought a bike on credit (of course) and off I went to practice. A neighbor that lived directly opposite to Emily's house sold motorbikes and motorbike gear. He took me out one day, to the shop where he worked and spent the whole morning helping me purchase my gear and choosing my bike.

Three months into my riding, I remember sitting on my bike at a set of traffic lights. I was afraid of having an accident on my motorcycle. I would get home, and my arms and legs were so sore from the tension. My neck and my back were suffering too. I had this huge conversation in my helmet that if I was going to be scared, then I should just sell my bike and do something else.

What was the point if I was going to be terrified every time I got on my bike? The whole reason to do this was to have fun, and so I made up my mind right there and then, that that was what I was going to do. I was going to let go and enjoy my experience. I had the most amazing trips on my bikes and met the most phenomenal people. Many are still our friends today. They are just lovely, genuine people.

Soon after I started riding, my cousin Sofia came over to my house to tell us the wonderful news that she was pregnant. One week later my sister was also announcing that she was pregnant. Perfect! That was just perfect! This news infuriated me. My cousin and my sister had spent most of their adult lives saying that they were never going to have a baby. I was always telling them how incredible children are, and here they were blessed with their baby, and I had none of my own.

What confused me at the time was that my sister's husband was only a year younger than Daniel, but he smoked and drank as much as Daniel. So why was she pregnant only one year after getting married? Anna's pregnancy made no sense to me at all at the time. I just remember thinking that life is not fair, it's not right, it's not just. I hated my life. Again. Nothing ever seemed to go my way. What was I doing wrong?

But there is so much evidence that shows that smoking and drinking alcohol lowers your chances of falling pregnant. Daniel had refused for years to quit because this is who he was when I met him. There was a lot of blame being cast this way and that way. When my sister fell pregnant, all of that changed. I started to question my beliefs. And yes, we had discussed many times if Daniel wanted to have children and he did.

From Daniel's point of view, there were hundreds of people that drink and smoke and they had babies every day. He was living proof of this theory. So I had to reassess my thoughts and feelings. I just wanted to give my child the best possible start in life. Why was that wrong?

By the time Sofia and Anna were six months pregnant, my parents decided that they wanted to return to Argentina. At least there, they would be closer to Anna when she had her children, and they could visit her more often from there. These last three months were hard for me because I didn't know if I would ever see them again.

So I tried to visit my parents as often as I could. Mom and Dad were now living with Emily, my mother-in-law, so at least they were closer. They had moved in with Emily shortly after Anna left for Miami. They couldn't afford to pay for the apartment my sister was living in with their pension, on their own.

I always felt that I had to be the strong one, and couldn't express my feelings because I didn't want my parents to feel obligated to stay with me or to have to choose me over my sister. She had no problems letting them know that she needed them all the time and so that is why I think they were always following her wherever she went. When I had returned to Argentina after my year here in Australia with my cousin Sofia, my sister went on and on about how my parents wouldn't stop talking about me and how precious I was. She had made me feel guilty that they should love me at all, over her, as she was always there for them.

Because of these comments from Anna, I decided not to make my parents feel that they needed to choose between us. They should be free to be wherever they wanted to be. I didn't want to guilt them into being with me, or want them ever to feel obligated to be with me. To them, it probably came off as not needing them and not wanting them.

I spent the next two years resentful because I didn't want to put my body through the IVF treatment. We couldn't afford this expensive treatment anyway. Believing at the time that the baby could not be as healthy as one that couple's conceive naturally. I was angry that everyone else was allowed to have children and some could have many kids, while I couldn't have one. It just so happened that in these next few months, Daniel quit smoking, which took the pressure off a little bit for me.

The following Christmas, Emily offered to pay for the IVF treatment. It took me ten months to make up my mind that I would at least give it a go. I did not go into the treatment with a heart full of gratitude. Gratitude that this treatment even exists and that we have other options when it doesn't happen naturally. I was not in a decent place. I was always angry with someone and sometimes with many people at the same time. No sooner had I forgiven one person when another person was on my offender's list.

We filled out all the paperwork for the IVF treatment, and the doctor took us through all the things that can go wrong. He also explained that our odds were quite low because of my age. I was more than forty, and apparently, that's old. Being too old to do things seems to be a recurring theme for me. I didn't feel forty years old. I had kept very healthy throughout the years and felt the strongest and fittest I had ever been.

When I was young, I was very athletic but not very strong. With the gym course and learning to ride the motorbike, you discover muscles you never knew you had. At this stage in my life, I believed that it was crucial to get strong more than fit. I wanted to keep my muscles and bones strong for when I got older. In my mind, I was nowhere near forty. In my head, I never aged a day past twelve years old. Always keeping it simple and finding the fun in every moment. Keeping my mind young, has helped me relate better to my students. Otherwise, I cannot understand how they process my lessons and what works best for each.

I started the hormone injections in November and all the blood tests that go with it. I produced fourteen eggs with this treatment! My doctor was taken completely by surprise. It was unbelievable that I could produce that many eggs at my age. The doctor implanted the fertilized egg just a few days later.

I was not happy. Nor was I excited about the idea that there might be a baby growing inside of me.

I was so angry that I had to go through this treatment and had to put my body through all this stress. Countless feelings were going through my mind, but none of them were joyful, peaceful or of gratitude. Anger, spite, resentment, envy. These negative emotions were poisoning my heart every single day.

When you fill out the paperwork for the IVF treatment, the doctor talks to you about what can go wrong, and Ovarian Hyper Stimulation is one of the many things that can complicate the treatment. Apparently, one in 1000 women is affected in this way. Well, guess who drew the short end of the stick? Surprise! Five days after my implant, I looked four months pregnant. By the weekend, I felt sick as a dog and had to go to the hospital. I couldn't eat. I would eat four spoons full of food, and that's all that would fit into my stomach.

My body was retaining water rapidly. The nurses weighed me when I entered the hospital on Sunday, by Friday I had gained ten kilograms in weight. My body had swollen up like a balloon. I looked seven months pregnant by the end of that first week in the hospital. On Wednesday night, I called Daniel late at night to please take me out of the hospital and take me somewhere else. I felt that the doctors didn't know what they were doing.

Thursday night, I thought I was going to die for sure. My left leg had swollen up so badly, I looked like the Michelin Man, and I hadn't urinated in one whole day. By this stage, I couldn't eat anything either as there was no room for food to go in. I was having difficulty breathing because my organs were pressed up against my rib cage.

That night the nurse that was taking care of me had to check on me every hour on the hour. She had to take my blood pressure and make sure that I was still alive. The nurse had been one of my students. Her name was Jenny, and I had also taught her dad for many years. Somehow, when I saw her face and I recognized her, I knew that everything would be okay. She was like an angel sent to watch over me.

On Friday, they had to remove all the excess water that my body was retaining. The doctor that drained the fluids from my body came down in a huff. He was in a rush and therefore blundered the procedure by operating on the wrong side. So they needed to do it a second time. The pain was excruciating, like nothing I had experienced before. When they had finished draining the fluids, they put a catheter in and sent me to another hospital that had more experience with cases like mine.

When I arrived at the new hospital, they put me in a room all by myself. I was terrified. Nobody had come with me because the hospital was one hour away from home. I buzzed and buzzed, but nobody came. This was the end of my life for sure. Here I would die, all alone. Eventually, a nurse showed up and asked me what was wrong. I told her that my buzzer wasn't working. She checked it and said it was functioning correctly.

I just wanted to know that there was someone there, as I couldn't get up and walk out of the room on my own. Without Daniel here with me, I did not want to be alone right now. All by myself in an empty room with nothing but the equipment making noise. Despite the former hospital being noisy, at least there was always a person in the same room with me. There was always a patient in the bed next to me if I needed to talk to someone.

I remember feeling alone because throughout this whole experience, nobody had spoken on my behalf to get me better treatment or better help. The first hospital I visited, had no experience with what was wrong with me. Daniel should have stood up for me. He should have fought with the doctors to send me somewhere better. Turning a hospital upside down is what my mom used to do. She had always done this for my dad. Ensuring at all times that he got the best care where ever he went.

I found out later that the hospital was under direct instruction from my IVF doctor. The doctor taking care of me in the hospital had contacted my IVF doctor on the first day of me being there. He had asked Daniel for his direct phone number. My IVF doctor was continuously telling them what to do next and what to look out for in my case. The doctor at the hospital genuinely wanted to learn about my condition. He wanted to help me and in turn, could learn to help other women that may end up with the same reaction to the IVF treatment. He was lovely. Another angel sent to take care of me.

This doctor said he had three children of his own and that he would do everything possible to help me keep mine, especially after he had heard our story and knew everything we had been through to have this child.

After ten days in the hospital, I could go home. It's funny. The people you expect would come and see you, are too busy to show up. The people you least expect are there for you. Most of my motorcycling friends came to visit me, and so did my neighbor. I was so grateful to have these friends in my life, as my family (my parents and my sister), were all overseas and unable to come and see me.

I had pushed away a lot of people in this past year because I was so angry at everyone and the world. My neighbor was the only person available to pick me up and bring me back home. It's funny that when you are in the hospital, all you want to do is be home with what you had. I missed my pets terribly and couldn't wait to see their little faces again. Seeing Daniel at the hospital practically every day was comforting, but it was not the same as being at home with him.

Six weeks passed very quickly, and I was asked to have a

scan to make sure the baby was okay. This scan is where you get to listen to the baby's heartbeat. I was so excited. It was the first time I had any hope that a baby was growing inside of me. I couldn't wait to hear its little heart. After all, I'd been through; it was finally my turn to hold my baby in my arms. The sonographer couldn't find the heartbeat, so they booked me in for a second scan.

The second scan revealed that there was no heartbeat, crushing my soul completely. This scan was on the 20th of December. Five days before Christmas. This was the darkest period of my life. I had nothing left to live for after this moment. Praying each night that I would not wake the next morning. Being unkind to so many people because I wanted them to know how much it hurt inside. Hating everyone and everything, just wanting it to be over.

As I remember this moment in my life, it fills my eyes with tears. It fills my heart with so much sadness. But it also fills me with gratitude. It is through this dark time in my life that I now understand how people can be unkind to others. The ones that hurt others the most are the ones in the most pain. I am so grateful for this experience because without it I could never have understood why people hurt others, especially their loved ones. Somehow, they are the ones you want to wound the most.

I wanted everyone to feel pain as much as I was. Saying hurtful things to my sister and my cousin Sofia. Pushing them away because at that time I had nothing to give. Since I felt empty inside and had nothing left to offer, hearing how wonderful everything was for them, just made me feel sick in the stomach. Knowing about any of their magical moments with their babies just infuriated me. I didn't want to know about anything. I'd wake up every morning thinking, "I give up."

Most of this Christmas and New Year's Eve, I spent crying.

I was in my forties and had no idea what to do with my life. It had no meaning. It had no direction. I just didn't care anymore, about anything, about anyone. No-one could take away this pain inside of me. No-one could replace my heart with a new one. Nothing I did gave me everlasting joy. Everything was fleeting. Everything was temporary. I had no peace, no joy, no love to give and now there was a dead baby inside of me.

All I could think of was that I wanted it out of me. It reminded me every day that I failed and wasn't able to take care of this baby. The first time, the only time, I had been able to have a baby inside of me, and it didn't survive. I had a blood clot in my left leg which meant that I needed Clexane injections twice a day in my thighs. These would give me migraines, which added to my depressive mood.

At the end of January, I had to have a scrape done at the hospital. It's the procedure where they clean you out, so the baby is no longer in there. I was slowly starting to get my strength back. Daniel threw me a surprise birthday party with my friends and family. All my cousins here in Australia came. It was wonderful. It had been ages since we had all been together. I got pretty drunk, which wasn't hard, as I'm not used to drinking.

My sister tried talking to me several times during this period in my life, and she said to me one day, "I know how you feel." The first thing I said back was: "I didn't know that you had lost a baby too, when did that happen?" Anna stated that she had never miscarried a baby, so I told her "how can you possibly know how it feels?" This comment made me want to lash out even more.

I have included this conversation just to let you know that when someone is in pain, sometimes, the worst thing you can say is "I know how you feel." Nothing you say can take away the pain that person is going through at that time. Just be there for them. Hold their hand. Listen to them. Give them a hug if they will allow you to. Let them know that you are there for whatever they need, so they know they are not alone. If they say nasty things to you, be patient. They are just going through their grieving process. Allow them their space to let out their pain.

People grieve in different ways. Some need support and hugs and kind words. They need to know that you are there for them, while others need to be alone. The quiet allows them the space to breathe. Some people just want to cry when they need to or yell out loud without having to justify why they did that. Only you can know what is best for you and the person in pain. Respect their wishes and when in doubt, just ask them what they want. Not what makes you feel better, but what they need from you. Ask them. Show them that courtesy.

There's a very significant moment I had in the hospital that I wish to include here. I was on the mend after my reaction to the IVF treatment. Having been in the hospital for about ten days now, one morning, I couldn't stop thinking about a cheese sandwich. Two slices of white bread a bit of butter and one slice of tasty cheese. It wasn't something I usually had at home, but for some reason, I was craving one.

I had already ordered my breakfast and lunch for that day, and there were no cheese sandwiches on the menu. That very afternoon, the tea cart pulled up asking if we wanted tea and biscuits. Not feeling hungry, I said, "no thank you." As I said I didn't want anything she had to offer, the cart lady asked me if I wanted a cheese sandwich. An elderly patient had ordered one but wasn't feeling well enough to eat it. I couldn't believe it.

Now I understand. God is with us at all times. Constantly reminding us that we are not alone, by sending us signs that He is with us. God cannot interfere with our life choices. Otherwise, we wouldn't have free will. There would only be His will.

Hollie Belle

In this chapter look carefully at your life.

Look at all the moments in your life where you have felt hurt.

Have you injured others because of this pain?

If you realize that you've hurt others because of the pain inside of you, make amends today.

Apologize to those you have hurt because of your pain. Explain the reason you hurt them.

This exercise is for you. If you can apologize and make the other person feel better that it was not their fault and that they didn't do anything wrong, this will free you of this burden. Otherwise, you carry this around with you. It makes you feel awful; it makes you feel guilty that you were horrible to another person.

To create an amazing, magnificent life, we must learn to get rid of everything that makes us feel bad. Everything that weighs us down. That weighs down our energy.

Understand that the other person may be very wounded by what you said or did. It may take a few times for them to get over what happened and that's okay. If this person is important to you, it will be well worth saying sorry as many times as you need to.

Also, I want you to take the time to sit quietly and look at the people who have hurt you. Can you see that they were suffering just as you have been? Is it possible that they wounded you because of the grief they were carrying inside of them? When you understand that you have hurt others because of the pain inside of you, then you can know how others have afflicted you due to their suffering.

Look carefully at their behavior. Examine the things they

said and what they did to you. Imagine for a moment, exactly how much grief would a person need to be in, to have done these things or said those awful words to you? What have they been through in their lives to have caused them to be so miserable? The moment you can see your pain and how this makes you interact with the world, then you can start to see this in others. It is like a domino effect. The world will never look the same again for you. Seeing the pain in everyone is where true freedom lies.

Chapter 9

WHAT ARE YOU WAITING FOR?

Desperately needing a distraction, I decided to start teaching a new course for little ones. I registered and did training so that I could provide music classes for little ones between the ages of two and four years old. I hired a hall near my home but found that there weren't enough students to justify paying for a room. So I cleared a space at the front of my house and started lessons there. This age group was such a joy to teach. There is so much to learn about toddlers and how they interact with the world. They are hilarious.

I made sure that nothing was pink so that the girls wouldn't all be fighting over this item. But then, if one little boy decided he wanted something yellow, they all decided they wanted the yellow one. Lucky for me, I had bought most of the instruments all in the same color. The tambourines were all blue; the bells were all green, etc. I had very few things in different colors, having already learned a little bit about this when I worked at the music school in Adelaide.

Just shy of ten months later, I felt strong enough to go back to the fertility clinic. Once our eggs were fertilized and frozen, the process was a lot easier for me. There was no need to go through all the hormone injections. It was so much simpler.

I wasn't going to tell Daniel that I was going in. I didn't want him to feel disappointed if it didn't work this time. He was still recovering from our experience in the hospital the previous year. My being frail and infirmed had left him a bit shaken up.

I had no expectations, but wasn't ready to give up yet. I had five fertilized eggs at the clinic. We could at least try those before calling it a day. I hadn't paid attention when my IVF Dr talked about all the hazards of the IVF treatment, just as being in your forties lowers your odds of falling pregnant considerably, went in one ear and out the other. I had stubbornness issues, but then this was my dream we were talking about here. It had been my dream for over fifteen years to become a mother.

Three attempts later, we finally had some luck with the baby implanting. Each attempt was six months apart from each other as I needed time to recover from the shock of losing another baby. Mentally, I just needed to prepare for each attempt as we tried yet again. There's always that little voice in the back of your mind telling you just to give up. Along with that other little voice that keeps telling you to give it one more try.

After they had implanted the baby, we needed to come in for the six-week scan. Unfortunately, after the last one, I didn't have the courage to go in for that one. So, I called in and said we would be away visiting family and that we would be back for the three-month scan. The first three months, I felt so tired and depending on what I had eaten, would be a little nauseous, but never needed to throw up. For the most part, I felt fine and discovered that if I felt woozy, going for a walk would make me feel better by the time I got back home.

At three months we went in to have our scan with the IVF clinic and found out that indeed a little person was growing inside of me. We both cried at the twelve-week scan. We were so thrilled that not only was the baby alive but that the odds of its survival were quite high. Everything pointed to the child being robust and healthy at this point.

At the twenty-week scan, we discovered that it was a girl. We were relieved because Daniel and I had always expected it to be a girl. We didn't have any boy names picked out. So we wanted to know if it was. That way we could spend the next twenty weeks agreeing on a name, or should I say arguing over one. How hard is it to both be happy with a boy's name? Well, every couple of weeks, we kept changing it. I think Oliver was the only name we were sort of happy with, but not 100 percent thrilled with this choice either.

Being pregnant was such a joyful experience for me. I loved feeling my little girl growing inside of me. It was the most amazing feeling in the world. I felt sorry for Daniel as I knew that he would never be able to have this experience. To feel a life growing inside of you. It was such a blessing that I wasn't sick and could enjoy all her little movements. My favorite memory was when she had the hiccups.

Whenever someone wanted to feel her, they would put their hand near my tummy, and she would stop moving. Almost like she could sense their energy coming towards her. When she had the hiccups, she couldn't stop, so it was easy for others to feel her through my tummy.

Being pregnant was such a precious time in my life. It was hard for me to let go and just love her and talk to her all the time. I felt apprehensive about getting too attached, in case she wasn't meant to be. At seven months, I discovered the book The Magic, by Rhonda Byrne. It is all about gratitude and being grateful for everything in our lives. This book gave me a distinctive glow. I felt different and felt happy for the first time in a long time. Honestly feeling full of gratitude for the first time in my life.

One of my friends, Diane, held a beautiful, surprise baby

shower for my little girl. She invited some of my students and friends. We had a lovely time. I now had plenty of things for when she would be born. Many of my neighbors and the parents of my students gave us items for our baby too. Before she was born, we had a cot, a pram, clothes, a change table, toys, pretty much everything we needed to get started. I couldn't believe all the wonderful things people had given us that they no longer needed. It was a fantastic time and the more grateful I felt, the more I received to be thankful for in my life.

Finally, the day came when she would be born. She was ten days late. I couldn't wait to meet her. It felt like I had spent my whole life just waiting for this moment. My entire life had been spent dreaming about her, wishing for her, longing to hold her in my arms and the time was almost here.

I had dreamed of a beautiful birth and being able to breastfeed her and the special bond that we would have as mother and child. Dreams of living blissfully ever after and finally, all my worries would be over. For so many years, I had imagined that when I became a mother, my life would be perfect. My life would be complete. We named our little girl Laura.

The big day arrived, and I ended up having a caesarean. My breast milk would not come in. Not being able to feed my child made me feel like such a failure. My breasts ached. I could barely touch them, and it was so painful to have the nurses handling them trying to get the milk to come in. Isn't feeding your child a natural thing to do? Doesn't your body just instinctively know what to do? Sadly, this is not so. I developed gestational diabetes throughout the pregnancy. Due to this, Laura had to be on a glucose drip for the first three days.

All I could think about was that I had to start teaching piano again in four weeks' time, how was I going to breastfeed Laura? Every midwife we spoke to, gave us different information and different advice. The breastfeeding period was a very confusing time for Daniel and me. I had to keep teaching piano as we needed the money to pay the bills and the mortgage. Lucky for me, I only had to work three hours every afternoon, and had very few adult students left throughout the daytime.

The whole situation just seemed impossible. We ended up feeding our little girl formula and giving up on the breastfeeding altogether. The harder I tried to get the milk to come in, the less I could produce. We even bought a very expensive breast pump to help get the milk to come in. My neighbor, Tania, helped me a lot through these times. She defended me in the hospital when the nurses were hounding me about the breast milk. Coming over whenever I called her, and helping me buy things that we needed. Throughout this whole time that was so confusing for us, she was a blessing.

Coming home with Laura was scary. I didn't have my mom to help me out and to give me advice when I needed it. The first two days back home with our new baby, I hardly slept and couldn't stop staring at her. What if something happened to her throughout the night and I wasn't there to save her? I frequently worried about cot death or her smothering herself in the bed during the hours I was meant to be sleeping. Now that Laura was finally here, I didn't want to lose her. I had so much love to give to her.

Three months later, I was teaching piano, and I felt a sharp pain in the middle of my chest. It felt like someone had stabbed me and left the knife inside of me making it impossible to breathe. I called Emily who was minding Laura, and she called my neighbor. Tania took me to my local doctor, only to find out that I didn't have a heart attack. Well, that was a relief! But still, the piercing pain in my chest was excruciating. Unbearable. My breathing was getting shallower and shallower. There was something seriously wrong.

When we arrived at the hospital, the doctors told us that my gallbladder had to removed. So another three months went past, and I had to go in for surgery, which was quite scary. Leaving behind a six-month-old baby to have an operation. Everything went to plan, and I was back home the following morning.

The first year felt like all we did was feed her, clothe her, and bathe her. Next, to Laura's crib, we set up a little bed. I am a very light sleeper. If she were in the bed with Daniel and me, I would get no sleep at all worrying that if we rolled over and squashed her, she wouldn't be able to breathe. Every time she woke up, I could hear her, and she didn't need to cry for me to come. I was just there.

Sometimes, all I needed to do was rock the crib a little, and she would go back to sleep. Then there was the teething. Joy! No sleep at all. When she turned one, she had four molars come out all at once. She had a fever and was irritable for a week until they all came through. Laura spent that night vomiting. It was a very rough week.

You know those babies that fall asleep in one spot, and you can pick them up and pop them down somewhere else to sleep, and they just keep sleeping? Well, Laura was not one of those babies. I had to walk her in the pram for hours so she could get her naps throughout the day. If the pram stopped, she woke up. At least, we were getting plenty of exercise. Grandma was helping out in the afternoons while I taught piano, so she was getting some exercise as well. Apart from that, she was a good sleeper.

Laura started walking at thirteen months. My little girl is four years old now, and I find that I am always learning from her and from the children she interacts with every day. There was so much I didn't know about children. The last four years I have been searching for answers. Why aren't I blissfully happy now that my daughter is here? It felt like I had waited my entire life just to have her and now she was here, it didn't feel any different inside of me. I felt full of love for her but no change towards everyone else. I thought my heart was going to explode with love and nothing would ever bother me again. Everything would be perfect.

I was angry with my sister and my cousin. After the death of my first baby with the IVF treatment, I had been unforgivably rude to both of them, and had apologized many times since Laura's birth. I tried explaining to them what I was going through at that moment in time, but explaining grief after such a devastating loss is impossible.

I could not understand how being my family; they didn't know that I would never hurt them intentionally. Shutting them out at that time, and not just them but the whole world, was essential to my survival. Unfortunately, others lose faith in you once they are hurt. They trusted you with their love and their feelings, and you push them away. The process of forgiveness can be quite slow depending on how much you have hurt the other person. Just be patient, hang in there. If you are sincere and these people are important to you, you will make your peace.

My belief that I was unworthy of being a mother had held me back most of my life, but my awakening has come from the fact, that here she was and I wasn't completely joyful and at peace with my life. She was born, and I was still angry with many people, and would be mad at even more people.

I believe the same happens with diseases. When we have had the same predominant thought about ourselves that makes us feel bad about who we are. Thinking bad things about yourself creates bad feelings. These, in turn, create tension in your body and eventually after many years of repeating this pattern, the body will manifest this with an illness. Your body is trying to tell you to change the way you feel about yourself.

Change your thoughts about who you are. I know what you're thinking, "What about a baby that is born ill, right?" Infants born sick are a different situation altogether. Hopefully, it will all come together for you in the end.

It was at this time that Daniel and I were having a conversation. He said something to me that stopped me in my tracks. I can't remember what we were talking about, but all of a sudden he told me: "You are still looking at your mother like you are five years old." That was it. Sometimes, the most valuable learning lessons come from the most unlikely of places. That's why you must pay attention to everything that is said to you. Sometimes, the people you least expect can give you the most valuable message.

So, there it was. I was stuck in a moment in time where my reality shifted. My perception changed, and it has been distorted ever since. I made up that my mother no longer loved me. She no longer wanted me and therefore replaced me. Tossing me aside like a toy she no longer wanted to play with anymore. All because she was now spending more time tending to my newborn sister.

From this moment on, I began to question all my beliefs. Realizing that every addiction (and we all have them), are a reflection of one truth. We believe that we are not good enough just as we are. We are unworthy of love just the way we are.

My whole life, I had learned to treat money like it was a separate thing. Detached, just like God was to me. You see some habits are evident that we feel unlovable: smoking, drinking alcohol, obesity, taking drugs, but the truth is that everything that we do that makes us feel bad is an expression of our lack of love for ourselves. It is our way of punishing ourselves for not measuring up, for not being perfect, for not being good enough.

My first step to awareness and mental clarity was ***knowing*** that I am not separate from God because He is in all things. The things we can see and the things that we can't see. Therefore God must be in me. Having an excellent sense of humor, sometimes the signs He sends me to let me know I'm on the right track, are amusing. He constantly reminds me that life is fun. Life is here for us to enjoy and not take it so seriously. Life is here for you.

Just as we are not detached from God, we are not separate from each other. I use the words **not separate** instead of connected because most everyone I know sees themselves as disconnected from everyone and everything, just as I did. That is why they see the world as unsafe and hostile. That's why we take everything as a personal attack. Everything is a reinforcement of how unworthy we are of love and how we aren't good enough.

The most amazing gift Laura has given me is that I understand my mother and her behavior. Having so much love and compassion for my mom now that I know what it means to be a mother. It is such a blessing, such a privilege, such an honor to have the power to create life. She has helped me to understand Emily as well.

Here is something I must mention. Emily would always come to see Laura with a gift, usually a toy. Bringing gifts is very common for grandparents and some parents. They feel the need to give their children things. Our house was full of toys because as I said earlier when Laura was born, we were given lots of second-hand toys from neighbors and my students. So she didn't need anything. I remember one day Emily coming in with yet another present, and couldn't help myself, I blurted out: "**You** are enough!" "**You** are what Laura needs." The fact that she sits with her granddaughter and plays with her and gives Laura her undivided attention. That's all Laura longs for and wants.

Many parents feel guilty that they don't get to spend enough *time with their children and they think that giving them toys will make them happy. These are just distractions from what your kids need: **your presence** and being fully present with them. Listening to them, playing with them, interacting with them. They need to feel that you see them, that they matter to you. That's all any of us have ever wanted. We want to know that we are loved. Loved for who we are, just as we are.*

As Laura was born, I took on the role that I needed to do everything, or it wouldn't be done properly. Again, my old habit of not trusting others. They will only let you down. The first year, it was tough to share her. I just wanted to be with her all the time, and if she cried, I would just pop her into my pouch and let her settle there. Not giving others the chance to soothe her because I just couldn't stand her crying. It felt wrong to me to just let her cry when I knew that I could calm her down quickly. Truth be told, having waited so long to have her, I found it difficult to share her with anyone. I felt resentment when others got to spend time with her. Time that I could be holding her, loving her.

Wanting to be a mother more than anything else in the world, my prevailing thought was always that my child knows that I love them. Nothing else mattered to me but wanting my child to know that I love them no matter what because I know the pain of feeling unwanted and unloved. Loving them exactly as they are. Not because they are smart or because they are brilliant at sports, but because they are my child and I have the privilege of caring for them until they are old enough to take care of themselves.

As she started walking and talking, she became more of a handful. You see nature takes care of everything. So it got to a point where it would be exhausting, and I needed help and was happy to share her to get that help. The good thing about being with Laura is that my days seem the same as when I was young. Each day seems endless now because we just go from moment to moment.

It would have been around this time that I sought out the help of a financial counselor. You see when you become a parent; something happens inside of you. Your children make you want to be the best possible person you can be. You don't want your kids to suffer the things you didn't like when you were growing up. Not knowing how to do this on my own, I found the help necessary, because my situation seemed bleak and hopeless to me. The finance counselor could teach me how to manage money or at least get me started.

After going over all the numbers and all our debts, we were only $40 behind every month. In other words, we were spending $40 more than we were bringing in. Daniel and I were on the lowest wages we had ever been on, so this was great news for us. Selling my motorbike which was under finance put us at an advantage. My bike was $75 per month plus $40 for its insurance. Things started looking promising.

He gave me great tips on how to put money aside each week for bills that come every three months or even for my annual bills. I learned to put a bit aside each week for Christmas. Even if it is just $10, it adds up to $500 by the end of the year. That's heaps to buy everyone presents. The important thing to take away from this is that no situation is too hopeless that you can't turn it around. Find someone who is skilled at what you want to achieve and seek their help. It is such an empowering feeling to learn to do something you thought you couldn't do.

I was able to do all of this, once I realized and accepted that I had an issue with money. More importantly, what that issue was. Not deserving to have money and not being worthy of all the wonderful things you can do and have with money was the underlying problem. I never learned how to manage money. Up until this point in my life, I never asked for help either. It was always my job to figure things out all on my own.

It has taken me two years, but the credit card is paid off entirely, and I feel that I can do this. I feel empowered now that I have learned how to manage my money. Becoming financially independent and abundant is possible because that is where my focus is now. We still have debt, but I am taking it one day at a time. It took many years to collect all the debt we have. Therefore, it will take a while to get rid of it. The same goes with obesity. You need to have patience with yourself. It takes many years to become overweight. It will take months and years to get healthy again when you decide to.

Another thing that I realized in this period of my life was regarding Emily, and I have to tell you this because so many people have these thoughts. For years before Laura was born, I kept thinking that if Emily passed away, we would inherit her house and her money. Finally, all our worries would be over. I had been playing the lottery for years and hadn't won yet. The truth is that it didn't matter if we did receive all this money because our relationship with money was not healthy. Our thoughts around money were negative.

My parents didn't have anything to leave behind of any value, so I didn't have these ideas about them. I had an awakening moment after Laura was born. As long as I kept feeling that I wasn't worthy of having money and that money was dirty, I would never be able to enjoy having it and living in abundance. The reason it had eluded me was my rejection for it in the first place. I had been conditioned for years to believe that money was wrong. That money was evil and only corrupt people have money, remember?

Then I came to the realization that the only thing that matters is people. Emily was far more valuable to us than anything she could leave behind. If we had her money, we wouldn't have her.

Teaching piano would have been difficult because there was nobody to mind Laura while I worked and Laura would have missed out on countless hours of playing with her grandma. She adores her grandma. Not only that, but Emily has been an incredible source of inspiration for me.

Our conversations and what we learn from each other every single day is priceless. We miss out on the valuable contribution that the person can make towards our growth and what we can give to them to help them evolve.

All of the memories I have as a child are about my experiences with various people. The happiest moments in my life had nothing to do with money. They have been a simple day at the beach. Playing in the snow for the first time with Daniel and Laura. Spending time with my dad and feeling loved by my mom. Holding my baby girl for the first time and she smiled the moment she was born. I think the only things that gave me joy that cost money were my piano and my motorbike. We focus on it like it is the most important aspect. More important than another person's life. Please don't feel guilty. Everybody has these thoughts.

One of my happiest memories was when my parents had to return to Argentina. I spent the night with them, snuggled up between the two of them. This was the only time in my life that I remember ever sleeping in the same bed as my parents. Playing tennis with Dad on Sundays when I was a kid. Eating Mom's homemade ravioli that would take her all morning to make from scratch. She had learned to make them from Sofia's mom. All the motorbike trips I have taken with Daniel. Just sharing my life with this incredible man has been wonderful.

I have to talk about money because for too many people, just like it was for me, their thoughts predominantly revolve around money. We are conditioned to think that money is the most important thing. Everywhere we are bombarded with you need cash for this, and you need money for that. You will feel better when you have a better car. You will feel better when you have a huge home with five bedrooms. All the while we feel inside that we don't deserve these things. All the while we feel that we don't deserve to be wealthy.

When you understand that you have always been worthy of all the beautiful things life has to offer, then you will let money flow to you. Understanding that you have been pushing it away because you don't feel good enough to have nice things is the first step. Your thoughts and your feelings about money are what have kept it at arms' length. I could only do all these things when I realized and accepted that I had an issue with money and more importantly what that issue was.

I mean, how many of you, feel comfortable when someone offers to buy you lunch or coffee? How many of you feel that you need to pay them back somehow? How many of you can't even accept this simple gesture and insist on paying for yourself? Shouting your mates with beer at the pub doesn't count, because you each take turns at buying a round. I mean someone just buys you a nice meal, and you can just accept it and say thank you, and you don't feel guilty that you owe them anything.

It is not enough to know that you have an issue, you have to look at what you believe about something to be able to turn it around. I thought that I didn't deserve to have money and all the spectacular things you can do with it because remember, only corrupt individuals have loads of cash. You can only be rich if you sell drugs or exploit others. Only bad people are wealthy, so it was not a good thing to have money because it meant that you must be a bad human being.

Now I challenge those beliefs. Why can't we help others and be wealthy at the same time? Why can't we enjoy beautiful things in our lives? Who decides if you are good enough to have everything you have ever dreamed of in this lifetime? You guessed it, **you**!

Think about it. When your electricity bill arrives, are you resentful when paying the bill, or is your heart filled with gratitude for this service? You can switch on a light, cook your dinner, have a warm shower, and keep your food fresh in the fridge. There are so many things that make your life so much better and easier because of electricity.

As I became focused on my daughter, I forgot about others that were in my life. I assumed that because they were adults that they could take care of themselves and look after their own needs. I was too busy with Laura. Taking care of her because she can't take care of herself, but I found that they needed my love and understanding the most and they needed my time just as much as she did.

Emily and I studied a self-esteem course together. In this course, they get you to look at your past and work out where you lost your confidence in yourself. We have both learned so much about ourselves, and it has brought us closer together as friends. When you start looking for answers, all sorts of astonishing things present themselves for you. Everything that has imparted itself in the last two years has been about looking at my past and finding the gift in every moment.

One thing I wanted to share here, was that when I felt frustrated, I would yell at Laura. After yelling at her, she would look so distraught, and it reminded me of how awful it felt when my mom shouted at me when I was little. I didn't mind cleaning up after her. It didn't bother me to pick up after her or clean up her mess. Her behavior was normal. She was just a little girl, having fun and exploring her world. I remember asking Emily many times, why did I need to yell at Laura.

The truth is that I was never angry with her for what she had done. I was annoyed that I couldn't pay a bill on time and had to pay a late fee or anything related to a lack of money. Other times it would be others that said things that made me feel inadequate as a mother. For example, that I couldn't get her to brush her teeth or brush her hair. How was she going to fit into society? She wasn't even three years old! This energy would make me irritable and less patient, and I would take out my frustration on her. Her mess was an excuse for me to vent because both of these issues made me feel like a failure.

I think too; the biggest problem was that I was still reacting to these events like I was the child that wasn't allowed to make a mess. The child that wasn't allowed to make a mistake and had to be perfect all the time. Getting smacked every time I did something wrong had conditioned me to react in a negative way to every time Laura made a mess. I promised myself that I would never smack my child or yell at them, as I know how horrible this feels.

Without this experience, I could never have understood what my Mom must have been going through in her life. All alone out here in Australia without family, without any help to raise me. My Dad was working such long hours to make ends meet. She must have felt frustrated that she couldn't do more to help him. I know because I felt that way about Daniel. Sometimes, it seems like the world is on his shoulders because I want to be able to raise my little girl. Taking care of Laura means that I need to work around her schedule and can't dedicate more time to work with my lessons.

I always let Laura express herself how she felt was comfortable for her. She wasn't big on giving hugs or lots of kisses, but she shows affection in many other ways. I believed, and I still do believe, that we are all different and we should be free to express ourselves in the way that makes us feel good. She didn't like being passed around like a football from one family member to another. She would cry and become uncomfortable, yet I've seen other babies go from one person to another quite happily.

It is not fair at this young age, or at any age to be comparing our children to others. Laura loves doing craft, and I hated doing drawing and painting when I was little. I used to find it tedious, and didn't see the point of it. It wasn't teaching me anything as far as I was concerned. She likes drawing, and so does her Dad and her grandma. We all love music in this house, and that is a good thing, but if she didn't like it, then I would need to respect her as an individual and accept her choices. We are not all here to become music teachers or musicians.

I believe that this comes from us, always comparing ourselves to others. We have all these ideas of what perfect looks like, but my question is always this: Who decided that? Who decided what perfect looks like in the magazines and on television? How should the perfect child behave? What should the ideal woman look like and how should she act? Or who the perfect husband and father must emulate? Who decided what the perfect male figure should be? We admire others for their qualities, but the truth is that these qualities are in all of us.

Everyone can be intelligent when they study topics that interest them. We all have the capacity to have an amazing body. Nothing is stopping you from dedicating more time to exercise. We all have the potential to look our best and feel good about ourselves. We were never meant to be the same as anyone else. That is why we all have different fingerprints and different color irises in our eyes. You have extraordinary gifts to give to the world, and I have mine. You are unique, and you are meant to be.

I remember when Laura was born and she was the most beautiful thing I had ever seen. There have been so many moments where I stopped myself and thought, "I don't deserve to have you." I don't deserve to have this much beauty in my arms, this much joy, and love. It would overwhelm me.

I had spent all these years waiting for Laura to arrive thinking that my life would be complete and that I would have peace. That all would be perfect and it wasn't. I figured something outside of me would make me happy. Something outside of me would give me what I needed to start living my life and stop making excuses.

I also spent many, many years before Laura, thinking that if I won the lottery, I would be happy. I would be complete. My life would take off. Now I know, that this is not true either. I already had the biggest miracle of all. My child and that wasn't enough. I knew it was time to look at myself and find the answers there.

Funny, I say that Laura was the biggest miracle, the truth is that my life is the greatest miracle. That I am here, is the miracle. I just realized that. Without my breath, nothing else would exist. I could not have created any of it if I did not exist in the first place. My Mom couldn't have me naturally either. She had to take particular medications that helped her ovulate more than one egg per cycle. Isn't that amazing?

In this chapter, I challenge you to look at your relationship with money.

How do you feel about money?

What are your predominant thoughts about money?

So many of us spend our days waiting for something magical to happen to be completely happy. In my case, when my daughter was born, everything was supposed to be perfect for me. All my anger would disappear, and all my feelings of rejection would miraculously go away. I waited my entire life for this beautiful little being to come into my life, only to discover that all those feelings I had about myself were still there.

Some people wait for their soul mate to make them complete.

Others wait for their marriage to end to have their freedom. Many think that retirement is the answer. When did we learn that happiness is in the future and that it does not exist right now in this very moment? Just like God was a separate being that lived way up high in the sky. He couldn't possibly be a part of me, nor I, a part of Him.

I dare you to look at your beliefs for what they truly are. Thoughts and words that have been passed down by others. For example, some parents believe that it is wrong to smack your children, while others feel that not smacking them is a lack of love. Some people let their dogs live inside the house with them. Others believe that the dog belongs outside. I am trying to get you to look at your life. How much of it is true? How much of it is lies that you chose to believe? It is time to let those lies go. But first, you must unveil the lies and see them for what they truly are.

For some people, this process will be extremely painful. Even gut wrenching. But what are your alternatives? To keep living the lies? To continue on the same path that leads to the same outcomes every single time? Although the process seems like hard work, it is far more arduous to continue to live the way you are. I know it is. Otherwise, you would not be here reading my words, looking for the same answers that I was searching for my entire life.

I know it seems, so cliché to say that the answers have always been inside of you. But they really and truly have been. Only you know what you have endured in your past. Only you know what you have chosen to believe about yourself. Therefore, only you can decide what the truth is.

I also challenge you to look at your life. What are you waiting for to be happy?

What do you feel you need to have or that needs to happen for your life to be complete?

STARTING THE PROCESS
OF HEALING

Well, here I am now and these past two years have been incredible. I think most of my growth has come in these previous two years of my life. Feeling so blessed with all the knowledge I now have, I feel it is my duty to point others in the right direction. I have spent most of my life looking for answers. Spending hours watching "The Secret" over and over again when it came out. Hoping that something would rub off on me and miraculously change my thoughts and the way I feel about myself.

Unfortunately, nothing came. No miracles of any kind except, of course, my bundle of joy that is now four years old. We call them bundles of joy, yet we should call them bundles of challenges. They just challenge you in ways you can't even begin to imagine. From your patience levels to your entire belief system. I thought being a mom was something that would come naturally to me. I was wrong. It is something that I have to work at every single day.

But I wouldn't change it for anything in the world. If you let your children show you the way, you will change in ways that you never dreamed were possible. Being a parent means being stronger than you ever thought you could be. It means suffering like you have never suffered before in your entire life. But it also means feeling like your heart is going to explode about fifty times a day because it just can't contain all the love that it holds for this one unique creature that has come into your life. While at the same time you also want to pull your hair out about fifty times a day because it's all too hard.

Everything that has happened in my life has brought me to this moment in time. It has brought me to you. To share my story with you, because as you wake up to what life is really about, you just want to share it with the world. You want others to wake up and stop wasting time on things that don't matter. Let me ask you a question, and I want you to be totally honest. If you knew that today was your last day to be alive, what are the things that mattered to you in your life? What were the moments that you wish you could hold on to forever? Which moments do you keep in your heart as the most precious?

Examining these last two years in my life, I realize that the moments of the most joy and the most love were all about the people in my life. Time we shared together. Either laughing or crying or just sitting in absolute silence. Moments with my mom when we played cards and watching her get cross because she hates losing. My Dad holding my hand and just giving me such a huge hug that his arms wrap around me and end up under my arm pits. I can't help but wriggle out because he ends up tickling me. Dad's voice. It's so gentle and loving. Boy did I mention my mom's laugh? It is so loud you can hear it from miles away. Her whole body joins in too.

My daughter has been my main source of inspiration. Through her, I can understand my mom, my mother-in-law and myself. The relationship between mother and child is unusually intricate and complex. Laura has taught me that I don't need to keep waiting for anything to be happy. It is all inside of me and always has been. Laura is happy with the silliest of things, and for the most part, it just involves her simple observation of the world. How everything she looks at seems magical and amazing.

Turning forty-five, I realized I was way off track. Here I was yelling at my daughter quite frequently. Making all the mistakes my mother had made with me and that I had promised myself I would never, ever do with my child. The only thing I hadn't done yet was the smacking.

I knew every time I got frustrated with Laura and yelled at her that nine times out of ten it wasn't about her. There was something inside of me that would snap at the drop of a hat. When you behave this way, you feel embarrassed that you can lose the plot so quickly.

How many times have I heard mothers say that? "I have turned into my mom." It is just habit. They find themselves saying the same things their parents said. So many years of living the same way have rubbed off on you. After your mom has said the same thing over and over again, it becomes embedded in your subconscious. I remember one day telling Emily that I am a horrible person because I yell at my child.

Then one day, I sat down quietly and looked at my life. I'm alright. I like who I am. So what's the issue with judging that yelling is wrong? The most important thing to understand was that my outbursts were never about Laura. They were about me feeling frustrated and angry. This was the first step towards clarity for me and consequently my freedom. Laura spilling things or making a mess was just an excuse for me to vent.

This led me to the biggest truth of all. Everything we express out into the world is about how we feel about ourselves. It is never about the other person. The more I saw it in myself, the more I could see it in others. Now when I had arguments with Daniel, I would hear him telling me that he didn't feel wanted.

Nobody was listening to him. As a result, he would explode, and we would end up having a heated conversation.

The words that people use to talk to you are not random. Listen carefully, and you will understand what they are trying to tell you. Most of all, I want you to start paying attention to the words coming out of your mouth. What are you telling others? Are you always tired? Are you always broke? Words have incredible power. Furthermore, start paying attention to your thoughts. What do you think about most of the time? As a matter of fact, the words that come out of your mouth are a reflection of the thoughts that plague your mind.

From here on, start monitoring either your words or your thoughts. Both of these are intertwined. Once you can see your patterns emerging, you will begin to see them in others. Focus on you first. Until you can understand what you are putting forth into the world, you cannot change. You will just continue to produce the same results.

Hopefully, by now, you know that you cannot change anyone else. You only have the power to change yourself. Once you start this process, nothing will be the same because you will be a better listener. Being more aware means that you can better communicate with others and guide them to their freedom and clarity. Also, you will be able to make others feel heard, wanted and appreciated.

Here I was turning forty-six and still feeling like something was missing. So, I answered an email that had been sitting in my inbox for over six months now. The guys I had done the self-esteem course with, were getting into health shakes and herbs. Their vision is that nothing is worth pursuing if you don't have your health to enjoy it. I totally agree with this concept, but at the same time, I believe that the past issues people are holding onto, will sabotage even the best of intentions.

I've watched my mom go on dozens of diets in her lifetime.

Only to fail, over and over and over again. When you are fit and healthy, you are addicted to feeling good. Enjoying that rush, you get when you have finished a workout, and you get this extra buzz of energy surging through your body. It is wonderful. But the truth is that if you are addicted to feeling bad, no amount of exercise or eating healthy will change that for you.

It will be a temporary fix, but it won't stick. You need to adjust your mind first. Fixing the thoughts that have derailed you every single time you have attempted to do something good for yourself. We've all been there. You get a little bit better; then you fall back into your old, familiar habits. The ones that make you feel that you aren't good enough and that you never will be.

Anyway, so I started network marketing and cold calling over the phone to sell health shakes. Committed to helping people get their health back. I realized that I was brilliant at connecting with people at a deeper level. I genuinely wanted to help them, but they all had the same issues. Lack of money and lack of health. Everyone I spoke to, was struggling with financial problems and they had some health condition. In total, I made 5,347 calls. Not one of these were happy and lived the life of their dreams.

Then one day I spoke to a lady called Rachel. She told me that she had worked at this massive production plant where they made these health shakes. She had been doing that for over twenty years. The fact was that the nutritional value of the shakes was not very good. It was very low quality. I was not impressed as these particular shakes were rather expensive.

I was distraught. You can't believe in anything anymore. Everything was a lie. I sought out the advice of my naturopath. I trusted her with my life. Karen told me that the product I was selling had below average nutritional value for the body. She had looked into it herself a few years before my visit and had asked for the complete list of ingredients with the quantities involved. Not only that, but the day I visited her, one of her students was there, and he told me how sick he got on the very same products. He suffered bloating and was almost anemic after six months of being on these particular health shakes.

My world came tumbling down. What now? How do I help others now? There were too many people suffering, and I felt I wanted to do something more. I couldn't give up now that I knew what was going on in the world. Rachel had placed me on a different path. She gave me a website to visit that helped people make money online. Of course, I was skeptical about the course. I mean, isn't everything on the internet a scam? But the course was only $20 a month, which works out to be $5 a week. Just a little more than a cup of coffee at the local coffee shop.

Not only that, but it came with a thirty-day money back guarantee. At this point, I felt that I had absolutely nothing to lose. If after thirty days I felt it was rubbish, I'd just get my money back. In fact, it was the total opposite. I have learned so much from this course. From putting together a website to creating videos. I am also learning how to put together videos to help people understand their past and change their beliefs about themselves. Hopefully, these videos are complete by the time this book is published.

The videos I have created include everything you need to help you change your internal programming. There are four layers to each video. Firstly, the words are printed out for you. I believe that words have so much power. How many times has someone said something to you, and this has caused you to be in pain for many years afterward because of these words? Secondly, I am reading the phrases to you. The reason for this is that you can feel my intention in every word that I am saying to you. My intention is for you to reach clarity. Clarity about who you are. I have created these videos with all my love for you.

My only wish is that you can feel the same freedom that I feel every single day. Knowing the truth is the only thing that can set you free to be who you are meant to be. Without worrying what others think, but understanding that we are all going through the same. The third component of the videos is images. The pictures will make a faster impression and have more impact on your subconscious mind. Lastly, there is music in the background. Music connects directly to the heart, bringing it all together. Images and music are direct links to the soul, as they do not need to be processed by the mind.

I had to go through quite a lot of pieces of music to decide which was the most appropriate. There was a beautiful piece with strings, but every time I listened to these, I wanted to cry. Eventually, I found exactly the right music. The music in the background now will help you feel light. It will make you feel like anything is possible because anything *is possible.*

Every moment that you are alive is a moment that you can choose to change everything, forever. The only way you can do this is by looking at yourself. Become the most passionate student of your life. Stop running away from what has happened to you and start embracing the fact that these moments, as difficult as they may be for you to face them, have made you who you are. You are you because of what you have experienced, as am I. I can't be here telling you my truth without all the moments that have led me to this one moment.

If I had never had Laura, I might never have awakened to this reality. I might still be in pain. If I were still with George, I might never have reached this point in my life. My life revolved around him and what he wanted and needed to be happy. Had I not met Daniel, and learned so much about him and his life, maybe I would have never put all this together. You are the sum of your experiences.

If you are here today reading my book, then this means that you are ready to wake up. You know that there is something more to life. More than just a nine to five job and scraping your way from pay cheque to pay cheque. More than just putting up with abusive relationships and rude people. Somewhere deep down you know that you were born for so much more than this. And you are!

Realize that running away from your past, burying it and trying to spend your entire life forgetting that it ever happened, will never work. Accept what you have experienced. Look at it for what it is. Try and look at it as if it happened to someone else. Someone that you love with all your heart, and you want to protect them from ever hurting again. What would you say to this person? What could you do to help them heal these old wounds? Thinking that your mother never loved you is awful, but it is more painful to keep reliving this event in your mind for the rest of your life. Believing that your father didn't want you, doesn't serve you either.

Some people cannot love. It is that simple. Their pain goes too deep that they cannot let others into their world. Not being able to love is their shortcoming. It doesn't have to be yours. If you didn't like what happened to you, then don't do it to others. Make a promise to yourself today that you won't ever make another person feel that way because you know how bad it feels. One thing is for you to have experienced it, another is to make someone else experience it through you.

Being a mother is a challenge. It is different to being a wife or a sister or someone's daughter. All of these titles require special skills. I wish I could help my sister see how wonderful she truly is, that she is caring and kind and beautiful. How she lights up Christmas and birthdays for all of us with her enthusiasm and cheerfulness. The same goes for my Mom. I wish she could see how I see her now. If Mom could only see herself through my eyes, that are full of love and gratitude for all that she has given me and for all that she is.

Over the course of the past two years, I have completed several self-esteem courses looking for answers. I've read many Louise Hay books trying to understand why I wasn't blissfully happy. Why wasn't I at peace? I was starting to resolve and manage my anger better, but I wasn't quite there yet. My bliss still eluded me. It was still out of reach. But I felt like I was doing everything right, you know? I should be feeling ecstatic about my life. What was I missing?

It wasn't until I started writing this book that I could see the truth. I could see with clarity. My life and everything that I have lived has been a gift. Until I could see and understand the present in every moment I have lived, I couldn't move on. There was no point moving on. I didn't want to keep living the way I was. Now, I just want to live a life of meaning. I want to know that what I say means something, that it can help others. What's the point of idle chit chat?

I want to say what I am feeling, and I want to know what others around me are feeling. How can I help them feel better about who they are? How can my presence be of benefit to those who come into my life? What can I do to help others see who they truly are? Being of service is all I care about now. Every conversation, I listen carefully. How can I contribute to that person?

Since I have been given so much, I feel that I owe others. Almost everyone we meet is struggling with personal issues, and practically all of them are memories that were created in childhood. Moments that we have held on to. Moments where we decided we were something that makes us feel dreadful about who we are. That's how this journey began. It was the realization that I had to find the exact moment in time where I chose to believe something about myself.

So I started writing them all down. Down to the very last memory, I could remember creating. Every single thought was made accountable, in the hope, that through this process of elimination; I could work out where I took a wrong turn. At what point did I come off the path of joy and confidence? Consequently, every moment after that has been about me collecting evidence. Evidence to prove my theories about myself. You can only go so far in your life when you still believe the lies about yourself. The lies that you created in your head.

This cleansing process as I like to call it began in the middle of my 45th year. It took me almost two years, but eventually, I had written down every single thought and memory I could recall from my entire life. Also, as I spoke to Sofia and Emily throughout this time, they would tell me about what they were going through, and some of these conversations reminded me of things I had forgotten about in my past. Meanwhile, as I was having all these light bulb moments about myself, I was helping them understand their past and their pain.

Strangely enough, when you share your thoughts and experiences, you help others gain clarity as well. Therefore I realized that this book could not be something that I kept to myself. In fact, once it was complete, I made three copies. I gave one to Daniel, one to Sofia and one to Emily. As the following year began to unfold, I kept getting a niggling feeling that this book needed to be accessible to more people. More people needed to know this amazing truth. So here we are.

MY MOM

This chapter is dedicated to my Mom. It is about everything I know about her and what I now understand. As I have already told you in my first chapter, my Mom lost both of her parents when she was five years old. I cannot know what that feels like and will never be able to know.

Becoming an orphan so young has made my Mom very possessive and very controlling, and that makes sense. She had lost the most important people in her life at such a young age. She also assumed that life is not safe. The world is a hostile place that just takes things away from you without warning or reason.

She is an incredibly brave and strong woman. Mom filled out all the paperwork to come out to Australia by herself. My Dad had no idea that they were leaving Argentina until they received their approval for immigration. She decided to move to a country where they didn't know the language. They had no idea what the culture was like, I mean, Australians could be eating their own young for all they knew. They took a leap of faith. Mom and Dad didn't have jobs in Argentina that they couldn't just leave behind.

My Mom did cleaning jobs in Argentina, and my Dad had

always worked in labor. She gave me all the love she could give me. Having lost everything so young, how could my Mom just give love, without being afraid that it will be taken away again? How do you love at all after such a devastating loss like that?

In addition to surviving this tragedy, the aunt that adopted Mom had no love to give her. All she had to offer my mom was just a roof over her head and severe beatings quite regularly as discipline. That was the way in those days. Never giving any affection or showing any real love. Otherwise, children grew up soft and wouldn't comply. How do you give love after being treated this way for so many years?

My Mom grew up in a house where they treated her like she was unwanted, unloved, a burden. It is so easy to judge others when we know nothing about them. Many days they went hungry because there wasn't enough food for all of them. Being ravenous in her childhood would contribute to my mom's obsession with food and many years of struggling with obesity.

We don't know anything about her aunt and the circumstances that she felt she had to take my mother in with her two sisters. Maybe she felt obligated, who knows? The truth is that my Mom did the best she could with how she viewed the world and I'm sure her Aunt did the same.

My Mom adores my Dad and yet I did not grow up in a house where they were overly affectionate to each other. Mom didn't like hugging and cuddling. It made her feel uncomfortable. (Then you wonder where I got it from as a child).

I watched my mom go on many diverse diets throughout my lifetime. She lost weight, only to pile on more weight when she had finished. You see, she never actually looked at the problem. The issue she had with food and what it meant to her. How this addiction made her feel bad about herself. It made her feel unattractive, and therefore it was easy to say, "How can you possibly love me?" Mom was hiding behind the exterior that she had created. Her obesity was like a force field surrounding her. She used it to keep others at a distance. It protected her from getting hurt.

She always showed her affection through her cooking. If she made something delicious that we loved eating, then she felt that she had given us her love. Her expression of how much she loved us was always evident. She just didn't know how to show her love in a way that was obvious to me.

I look back at all my childhood photos, and my clothes were exquisite. I even had gorgeous shoes to match. Parents that don't care don't go to all the effort to make sure that you look so cute. She expressed her affection in a million little ways. I couldn't see them because I had decided early on that she didn't want me anymore. That love was not safe. Love can be taken away, just like it had been taken away from her.

Throughout my childhood, I saw my Mom through her eyes. She looked huge to me. Being an adult you already look quite big to children, but being overweight makes you even more so. I saw her the way she saw herself. She was always cranky and yelling and upset. I could not see the beauty in her that I saw in my Dad.

The beauty I talk about has nothing to do with how handsome he was on the outside, although he has always been a very handsome man. I spent most of my life wondering what he ever saw in my mom. How could he love Mom, when he was so perfect?

One of the beautiful memories I have of my Mom were of her singing throughout the house when she cooked, or she was cleaning. I loved hearing her sing. It meant that there was something beautiful inside of her, she just didn't want us to see it.

She doesn't know that what we are looking at has nothing to do with what we see outside. We see her strength, we see her courage, and we see how much she cares for all of us. She would gladly jump in front of a moving vehicle for any of us because she always felt that our lives were worth more than hers. She felt that she didn't matter as much as we did and that was not true.

We all matter.
We are all worthy of love.

Growing up she taught me that books are your best friends because you can learn anything and everything from them. When my first piano teacher broke my heart, she told me that there was a male dancer that started learning ballet at the age of sixteen and he was very famous, and he danced beautifully. She taught me not to listen to others and their negative talk. That was their issue. It didn't have to be mine.

She taught me what courage was. In every hospital that my dad would have his heart operations, she would turn the place inside out if she felt that they weren't taking care of him properly. My Mom was fearless when it came to defending us. She had no problems standing up for any of us if she felt she had to.

She taught me never to settle, so if I was unhappy in a job, I should just quit and look for something else. So much time is spent at work, that we should be able to enjoy doing it, even though she had never had that privilege. The jobs she spoke of in Argentina, she genuinely enjoyed cleaning for her employers. My mother always talked about them with love.

My Mom was mainly the one that kept pushing for me to have a University degree because she wanted me to be well off and never have the financial burdens that my parents had to endure. She was quite a pioneer in her day. All my cousins learned that you get a job and then stick to that job because you need to make money. Earning money meant hard work for them and you didn't necessarily need to enjoy your work. So I am so grateful for Mom's wisdom.

She could see something in me that I couldn't see myself. She could see infinite possibilities for me. Opportunities that they never received as children. Possibilities that they could give me because we were now in Australia and everything was attainable here. All because she was brave enough to take that risk and get on the plane to come here with my dad. I guess, they had nothing to lose by trying, because they had nothing.

We always had a birthday cake made from scratch by Mom for every single one our birthdays. Mom was always trying to learn new ways to make them more and more beautiful each year. Christmas was special because Mom put up the tree and the lights and would decorate our house so that it was magical for us. She loved us with all her heart, but didn't feel worthy of our love. She never considered that she deserved our love in return, not even my Dad's.

As I write this chapter, I can't stop crying. How could I not see all of this before? How could I not understand that she did love me? All I've wanted my whole life was to know that she loves me because I have always loved her so much, but I always felt that she didn't want my love. She wanted my sister's love instead. Maybe because I was so different to my parents and my sister was so similar to my mom.

They both have so much in common. Both Mom and Anna love cooking. I lost interest after a few attempts to make unique dishes as they either came out burnt or not fully cooked. My first pizza was so salty that it was inedible. Instead of a teaspoon of salt, I put in a tablespoon. Oops! Granted, I'm not very good at following recipes. I always mess them up. Being allergic to following recipes is probably why I don't enjoy cooking at all. At least with piano I can make all the mistakes I need to, and I don't have to throw anything away if it doesn't work out. It felt wasteful when the food had to be thrown out.

Now that I am a mother, I understand that your children are all a part of you and that each child has a place in your heart that is equal to the amount of love that you have for them. Some of your kids are very different, and that is for your personal growth. They are there to challenge you to look at yourself and the world differently. Having our views challenged is the reason we are not the same, and we are not meant to be.

One important lesson you can learn from your kids is patience. Other lessons include do not sweat the small stuff. Learn to live in the moment. There is no tomorrow to a toddler, and there is no yesterday. Tomorrow to them can be in five minutes or two weeks. They have no concept of time at all. All they know is this moment right now. Just trying telling a three-year-old to hurry up because you're running late. Good Luck with that!

My Mom was spontaneous and impulsive. She would get an idea about something and just go with it. She never sat down and measured up the pros and cons with anything. That's how Mom and Dad ended up in Australia. Mom opened up her bakery in Argentina when I was twenty. I think after many years of caring for all of us, she needed something for herself. It was incredible. We learned so much. I admire that so much in my Mom that she would just go forward never worried about the consequences. As a result, we've had some amazing adventures because of her. She was never a "What- if" kind of person. She was always the "What have we got to lose?" kind of person.

In my childhood, Mom never let me go on any of the school excursions or camps. I couldn't go to other schools to play sports or sing in the choir at halls or events. She was very over-protective, but I love that about my mom. Due to this extreme possessiveness, I was safe. My Mom cared and looked after me, what more could I ask for when I had everything I needed for my personal growth?

Through Mom, I learned how to live in fear. The world is a hostile environment, and you will only get hurt out there. Also, learning how quickly things are taken away from you, including love. Lately, I've been thinking a lot about the fact that she grew up feeling unwanted and she passed that on to me. I wonder now if we feel strongly enough about ourselves in a certain way, is it inevitable that we will pass this on to others?

I spent years treating others like they were invisible and unwanted because that is how I felt. How can you make others feel good about themselves when you don't feel good about who you are? As an example, I grew up with my parents getting on well with my aunts and uncles here in Australia and then they would get offended about something and wouldn't talk to each other for years. Not feeling good enough for each other was the reason for this behavior.

This pattern has repeated itself throughout my entire life. Watching Mom and Dad waste years not talking to their siblings. It went both ways, though. Sometimes it was my aunts and uncles getting offended and not talking to my parents. And sometimes it was my parents that decided they didn't want to see them anymore because they made Mom and Dad feel bad.

More often than not it was because they didn't like the way their siblings had behaved and this would trigger not wanting to see them. They would pull out the "We don't deserve to be treated that way" card. Apparently, when I had pushed Christopher back as a child, he went crying to his mom, and she got upset. We didn't see each other for a year after that. It's funny because my Mom had witnessed him pushing me over for months and just told me to push him back. Go figure.

Also, Mom felt that she was alone in the world. Having

nobody to protect her, made her fearless when it came to confronting others. Mom had spent her entire childhood standing up for herself. There was nobody to defend her or protect her. She would tell off a surgeon or professor or anyone. Mom didn't care if you had a degree or who you were. You could be the President or the Queen. To her, if you weren't doing your job when it came to us, you were going to cop an earful from her.

I have all of those qualities in me. To me, you are a human being first. Whatever title you have acquired along the way doesn't give you the right to treat others unkindly. Some people believe that you need to have a degree to be somebody. So if you are a doctor or a lawyer, you have the right to look down on others. Supposedly, you are a superior human being because of your title, but this is no different to what we have been talking about in this book. Feeling superior to others is just another way of saying that you are not good enough. You have acquired that degree to make yourself feel above the rest because without it; you felt worthless. With no value at all.

So few people choose a career out of love. Usually, the reasons for obtaining a degree have more to do with self-worth rather than passion. That is why you often meet doctors and dentists that are rude and obnoxious. Their titles were merely to make them feel that they are somebody now. They were a nobody before their degree.

I know because this is what happened to me. Sitting in my classroom in my third year at University, I just knew that I was doing it for everyone else. It wasn't what I wanted to do with my life. I just didn't want to be a nobody. I believed that this would validate my existence. Having a degree would prove that I was smart and it would demonstrate that I deserved a place in George's life at that time. A person with a degree does not belong with a nobody.

With time I understood that my love was enough. Love is all you need to be happy. For all of us. He had chosen to share his life with me and all the while I just believed that I wasn't good enough. That somehow, I was beneath him. My parents were equals. Neither of them had secondary education, and yet, the wisdom that they passed on to my sister and me is invaluable. I get my strength from my mom, and I know that when I need to, I can take care of my needs.

Recently, I remembered my time in the hospital after the IVF treatment. When I needed things, I just asked for them. The nurses didn't want me to have a lounge chair that was in the waiting room, but I couldn't sleep in the bed. I found it difficult to breathe when I was lying down. After the third night of not being able to sleep, I refused to give back the chair. If I was going to die, I was going to be comfortable, damn it!

I encourage you to look at your relationship with your mother as you were growing up. If you didn't have a mother, then a maternal figure might have been present in your childhood.

Go through all the memories you have with this person. All the precious memories and all the memories that you feel were not so great. Try to look at them from behind *their* eyes. What was their childhood like, do you think? Did they seem happy? Were they kind to you? Did they express their love towards you in a way that you understood?

Also, how many of their traits have you taken on board? How many of their beliefs have become your own? What influence has this person had on who you are today?

Chapter 12

MY DAD

Growing up, my Dad was my hero. He was unconditional love and was everything I wanted to *be* when I grew up. He was my rock, and I thought he was the most beautiful man I had ever seen. I could rely on him for everything. I knew that he worked very long days to provide for us and make sure we had everything that we needed. When I was with Dad, I always felt safe and protected. No harm could come to me when we were together.

One memory I have was that I had burnt a tea towel and I knew my Mom would smack me for that. I went running to my Dad in tears, and I told him that it was an accident and that Mom would be outraged. He said not to worry. When Mom came home, he told her that he had accidentally burnt the tea towel himself.

I could talk to my Dad about anything and everything. The only reason I never asked him about sex was that the church had made out that it was such a bad thing to discuss. My Mom reinforced that at home, so I assumed that it was something that should not be spoken of at all with anybody.

I remember one day, my Dad came to me with a wooden box. It looked horrid to me. He looked so pleased like it was the most special gift ever. I said that I didn't want it. My sister saw the look of disappointment on my Dad's face and said that she would have it. That tatty looking wooden box was full of coins. I don't know if my sister had seen him putting the coins in or if she genuinely cared that I had hurt his feelings. To this day, I wish I had taken the box. Even if it was empty, it was important to him.

I had grown up with presents needing to be new and shiny. I wasn't aware that some gifts, the best kind don't come in specially wrapped boxes. Some don't come in packages at all. I wish that Dad knew that not a day goes by that I wish I had said yes to that box just because it came from him. I would still have it with me today.

He had also grown up in total hardship. Food and clothing were scarce in his childhood. They also went hungry more often than not, and they weren't gifted with love and affection because his parents were worried that it would make them soft and stray from being good people that fit into society. He copped terrible beatings as well, but he knew what love was.

Up until recently, I had a discussion with Daniel about caring for your loved ones. My Dad has spent most of his life telling my Mom to stop overeating. He was naturally worried about her health. Being overweight means that your organs are straining to work under all the pressure of the extra fat surrounding them. Dad has always been strict about what he eats and has always been lean.

My Mom would eat more. Telling her that she had a problem with food only made it worse. It didn't help her with her issues. But this is what love looks like according to Daniel. You advise your partner that they have a problem thus demonstrating to them that you care. My Dad still loves her enough to keep telling her that she doesn't need to do that anymore, even today.

Observing my Dad's behavior, I also learned that no matter

how much you love someone, you cannot help them. You cannot change them. He spent many years trying to help Mom with her weight issues. I remember going to shops to buy clothes with Mom and how embarrassed she felt if they didn't have the clothes in her size. Back then, we didn't have all the plus sizes that we have today. I think the largest size was eighteen and twenty. The bigger she became, the more difficult it was to find clothes to fit her.

My Dad, on the other hand, was a workaholic and I think this was a distraction to him. As long as his mind was on his work, he didn't have to think about anything else. Many people do this. While you occupy your mind with work, you don't have to look at yourself. You don't have to deal with the fact that you believe that you are unlovable or not good enough.

He made time to play tennis with me when I was older, and these are memories that I will treasure forever. We went fishing and camping with my uncles and cousins when I was older too. Before I started Catholic School, we stayed up late watching old movies in black and white that were running at night. After starting Catholic School, I had to go to bed at 8 pm. I had a digital alarm clock that would sit next to my bed, and I would lie in the dark staring at the ceiling until 10 pm. Alone with my thoughts for two hours. I wish I could have stayed snuggled up on that couch with my Dad forever. I felt happy then, and I knew he loved me.

Thanks to my Dad, I know what love is. Sometimes his love would shine through his smile. Other times it radiated through his eyes when he looked at us. Sometimes we could feel his love when he was just holding our hand or giving us a hug. There was never a doubt in my mind that he loved me just as I was.

With Dad, I learned what real love looks like between a husband and wife. He never raised his voice to any of us.

Whenever an argument broke out, he was the first one to disappear. Dad hated fighting and disagreements. Always being so kind to my Mom, complementing her delicious cooking. Making her feel special whenever possible. He never said anything mean or nasty to my Mom. In his eyes, my Mom was perfect.

When my grandmother stirred up trouble with her gossip, Dad just didn't want to take sides with anyone. He never defended my Mom against her, but then again, he never told my grandmother that she was right. Dad just stood on the fence line, and that is what got him into trouble with my Mom. She thinks he should have told his Mom to butt out. As a result, my Mom suffered immense stress because she was trying too hard to please everyone. Putting up with my grandmother's criticisms and judgments, almost caused her to have a nervous breakdown.

Due to having lost her mom so young, my Mom put up with my grandmother being unkind. She believed that whatever time we had together with our grandmother was precious. Eventually, Dad had a big talk with his mother, and I remember he was distressed because he made her cry. Upsetting his mom, caused Dad unimaginable grief and remorse when our grandmother passed away.

Dad was always making practical jokes and making us laugh. It was such a joy to be with him because he was funny and goofy. My Dad was what I called the "soft." My Mom was the "hard." She would bulldoze anyone that got in the way of her family. My Dad was a total pacifist. A man of few words when it came to arguments. Arguing didn't accomplish anything according to Dad.

Now, this is where I side with Daniel. If you don't put forth different views of the world and different opinions, how can we grow? Sometimes, people will say something to you that will propel you into new directions just because they see the world in an entirely opposite way to you. Just because they took the time to show you that maybe there is another way to look at things.

From my Dad, I learned to run when things got too hard, especially from confrontations. In truth, without confrontations how can we learn to look at things differently? Through my Dad, I found out that arguments were just a way to prove that you are right and the other person is wrong. Disputes did not create solutions in my Dad's mind, only rifts in relationships. In his mind, this is how war starts with each party trying to prove their point of view.

As a matter of fact, I can understand my Dad's thinking. You can't change someone else's mind. You can't force them to believe in something because you have no control over the thoughts that reside in the heads of other people. Forcing your beliefs on others or trying to prove them wrong doesn't accomplish anything. Many of the things I have learned in this life is because Daniel has been kind enough to share his unique perspective on things. His experiences have been so different to mine that he always challenges me to question what I believe.

More often than not, I change my mind about things. The thoughts I previously had on certain topics no longer serve me. All this, because Daniel shared his way of thinking. The issue with Mom and Dad was not knowing how to say what they thought, and feeling that others would reject their ideas. As children, no-one asked them what they wanted or what they needed. Nobody sat down with them to ask them their opinion on anything. Adults expected my parents to follow orders, and if they didn't, they suffered the consequences.

When my Dad met my Mom, this must have been the first time that someone listened to him. The first time someone cared about what he thought and what he felt. His first actual connection to another human being. The same must have happened to her, and that is why they are still to this day, so in love with each other. Until they met each other, they were unwanted and unseen. All it takes is one person to make you feel special. Just one. One person that makes you feel that you matter and that you are worthy of love.

They have gone through life with their past issues still intact, and this is what has helped me so much to be able to see mine. It has enabled me to see my problems and how these have affected my entire life. Hence, I can now see the patterns that Mom and Dad put into place for themselves as well. Mom with her obesity. Dad with his addiction to work and always keeping busy. They both had an addiction with debt.

When we are born, we copy everything that our parents or carers do. It is all we see. So naturally, we are going to imitate what is surrounding us. You learn to speak from listening to the same words over and over again. You learn to walk or do certain actions because you are observing those around you behave in this way.

Dad taught me to question everything. As his view of God was so different to my Mom's and the church, this made me doubt what I learned. I knew deep down inside that we didn't just die and the worms eat us. The End. I knew that there is a spirit inside of us that lives on. He taught me not to believe everything the church was telling me, especially the bit about being separate from God or a peculiar old man in the sky playing with people's lives like they were ants. Having my own thoughts about God and life was okay. After all, I couldn't prove Dad was wrong any more than I could prove Mom was right.

I felt that because Dad didn't believe in what the Church said, that I had the same privilege. They could not control my mind. I could have faith in whatever I chose to believe in. He taught me that even though you may have been born into a world of suffering, that this need not mean that you have to suffer your whole life. As an adult, you can choose to live a life of love even if you weren't gifted with love as a child.

He showed me how you could turn it all around. He showed me that you could stop the cycle of abuse in its tracks. We each have a choice, whether to continue the pattern passed on to us or whether we want to give out something better, something that comes from love. We can be the change we want to see in the world. It starts with us.

My Mom had chosen to keep living in fear. Fear of losing even more. Like losing both of your parents as a child isn't enough. My Dad decided to live in love. He chose to love my Mom with all his heart, and he was committed to loving us unconditionally. Dad loved his life, and I could always feel his gratitude for us. He felt so lucky to be our Dad and take care of us. Consequently, he never misses an opportunity to let us know how important we are to him.

I encourage you to look at your relationship with your father as you were growing up. If you didn't have a father, then a paternal figure might have been present in your childhood.

Go through all the memories you have with this person. All the positive memories and all the negative ones. Try to look at them from behind *their* eyes. Was their childhood a happy one or was it full of hardships? Did they seem at peace? Were they kind to you? Did they express their love towards you in a way that you understood?

Also, how many of their traits have you taken on board? How many of their beliefs have become your own? What influence has this person had on who you are today? Most of who you are is because of the people who raised you. They have molded you into the person you are today.

Try to examine all the things this person taught you and look at how much of it is true and how much of it is just stuff that has been passed down through the generations.

MY SISTER

My sister was the greatest gift of all. She taught me what it felt like to be separate from everything in the world. Then the church taught me that I was separate from God. So I was completely detached from everything and everybody. Her existence pushed my perception into an alternate reality. Without her, I would have been the center of my universe at home. But like I have said many times in this book, every relationship that you have in your life is a gift to you.

My sister was the opposite of me. Expressing her feelings was not a problem for Anna. She was very emotional, which meant that she would cry at the drop of a hat. Anna didn't like reading or learning but liked making things with her hands. She had no idea how to entertain herself. Constantly looking for others to keep her company. She didn't like sharing her toys or her possessions, but she was quite happy to play with your toys and use your stuff.

My Mom was always comparing her to me, and that could not have been good for her self-esteem. She is kind and caring and very aware of other people's feelings which place her one step ahead of me. I am only just starting to see others and their pain now. She was always expressing her feelings, whereas I learned that it was wrong to do so.

I dealt with Anna the way I felt inside. I acted as though she was unwanted by me. Acting as if she was invisible and I didn't care if she was there or not. Not because I felt that she deserved to be treated this way, but because she was the reason that I was treated this way. As she was getting all of my mom's love and attention, she didn't need any of mine. None of this was intentional or deliberate. It is how I am viewing the events today, recognizing my behaviour and understanding the reason for my actions.

As sisters we have never been close. Sharing so many years together, we have had moments, but they are so few and far between. My relationship with George would have severed anything we could have had, because he was always attacking her and I, never once, stood up for her. I was afraid that if I stood up to him that he would leave. He would walk away. In my mind, he was my future. Anna was my past.

She made me aware of all the things I wanted to forget about myself. Having to remember every day that I was no longer loved and wanted. Reminding me that I wasn't good enough for my Mom's love just the way I was and that I needed to earn this love. She reminded me of how fragile love is and how quickly it can be taken away.

I was incredibly cruel to her after my attempt at IVF. I felt that life was so unfair. She had spent her whole life saying that she wasn't going to have children, and here she was pregnant for the second time, and I couldn't fall pregnant at all. I had always loved children so much. It felt like she was an easy target. Maybe I wanted to give back some of the pain she had caused me when I was a child. I had not yet reached the point of clarity in my life that I now enjoy every day.

The last thing she said to me was "I know how you feel." I

responded with "I didn't know that you had lost a child." She said she never had and I just lashed out. How dare she say she knew how I felt?

I am telling you this because so many people seem to think that you make others feel better with those words. Sometimes, it is the worst thing you can say. Because unless you have been through the same experience, there is absolutely **no way** on earth that you can understand how it feels.

How it feels to go year after year, Christmas after Christmas praying and wishing with all your heart to have a child. Only to find that it never comes. For some women, this child never comes. I can't imagine how heartbreaking that must feel.

Instead, the best thing you can say to another person that is suffering is the **truth**! I have **no idea** what you are going through, but you know what? I am here for you. If you want someone to talk to or if you just want someone to sit with you and not talk at all. If you need help with house chores while you get back on your feet or need me to take your dog for a walk, I'm here to help. Show your love in ways that count.

Some people when they are in pain, it hurts them to be touched. For others, just being hugged feels like someone cares. Only you can know what is right, and sometimes nothing will be. Just let that person grieve in their way. If they need to vent and lash out, give them their space. If they say something hurtful and you get offended, here you have an opportunity to ask yourself, "Why does that upset me?"

After saying a lot of hurtful things, I have had to spend many times saying sorry to my sister and trying to explain the pain I was feeling at the time. She has never really forgiven me and hardly talks to me. I know in my heart that I didn't do the right thing by yelling at her and telling her off, but have made every effort to apologize on numerous occasions and will continue to do so until she knows that it was never my intention to hurt her.

My sister is worth it. I owe everything I am to her. I love her, and one day she will know this. She won't have to feel that she needs to compete for my mother's love. She will understand that there is more than enough love for all of us.

I remember my Mom always saying to her, "Why can't you be more like your sister?" Your sister doesn't complain. Hollie loves reading, and she always gets good grades at school. She plays quietly by herself and can keep herself entertained for more than five minutes. I want to dedicate this chapter to all those siblings out there that grew up in the shadow of their brothers or sisters.

It can't feel good if you're frequently told that you aren't like someone else, or as good as someone else. For the longest time, I thought my sister was jealous of me, and I couldn't understand why. Now it makes perfect sense. My Mom was always comparing her to me. While you compare, you are not accepting that person as they truly are. Therefore, you are not looking at all the good things that person has inside them. You are too busy telling them what they are not, rather than showing them all the wonderful things they are.

You are unique. You have come into this world with your unique gifts. We did not all come into this world to become brilliant mathematicians or top athletes. We didn't all come here to compose music or paint masterpieces or cure cancer. Everyone has their unique path to follow.

I honestly believe that if you can help one person. Just one person. Assist them to see their value, their worth, their beauty. If you can show them love and help them find their path, then that is enough. If that is all you get out of my book, then I have achieved what I set out to accomplish. To help you find your truth. Find your answers and therefore set you free. As a result, you will want to do the same for others. You will want to help others follow their hearts and hence, their true calling.

We spend so much time looking at what we are not and forget to look at what we truly are. Stop comparing yourself to others. Stop trying to be someone else and try to remember who **you** are. Remember what you like to do. Think about the things that make you happy. Think of all the things that fill your heart with love and excitement.

Now, sit down and look at why you aren't doing all this stuff. What is stopping you from living that life? Look at my story and my relationship with my sister. We were both more or less messed up. My sister was trying to live up to my mom's expectations that she could be as good as me academically.

Meanwhile, I felt tossed aside just because my sister was born and she seemed more special to my mom. Especially relevant is the fact that neither of us was truly happy. We were both fighting our own demons.

I encourage you to look at your relationship with your siblings as you were growing up. If you didn't have a brother or sister, maybe you had friends or cousins that might have been present in your childhood.

Go through all the memories you have with these people. All the cherished memories and all the memories that you feel were unpleasant. Try to observe them from behind *their* eyes. Did they have a happy childhood? Were they kind to you? Did they express their love towards you in a way that you understood?

Also, how many of their traits have you taken on board? How many of their beliefs have become your own? What influence have these people had on who you are today?

Chapter 14

DANIEL

Daniel has been my greatest teacher. Just like my dad, he is an atheist and is repeatedly challenging my faith. He is very insightful and is always helping to push me outside of my box. I never thought that it would be him that would start me on this journey with just one comment: "You are still looking at your mother like you are five years old." This observation has been the greatest gift in my life.

This remark was a turning point in my life. Since that moment, every time I have an argument with someone now, it feels like I am having an out of body experience. I see them talking about themselves with every word they say. I can recognize their pain. Their journey of unworthiness and not being good enough. I no longer take it as a personal attack like I used to in the past. Listening to them, I hear them telling me their story.

Daniel has been one of my greatest gifts. He gave me Laura which makes him invaluable to me. I will forever be grateful to him for this blessing. I started off in this relationship thinking that it was just temporary and look at that. We have been together for over twenty years now. My freedom and my inner peace have been thanks to him. My clarity, I owe it all to him.

That is why it is imperative that we don't turn up our noses at anybody because the most important message for us could come from anyone. Everyone is a messenger. Everyone that is in your life has something to contribute to you if you will but listen carefully.

Sometimes we learn things from others. Many times we discover what we don't wish to be by the example of others, like my first piano teacher. What I find fascinating, is that Daniel would have been the last person I would have expected to have pushed my button to force me to look at my life. Seriously! I know he's my partner and all that, but I've never thought of him as insightful. He was the one that said what I needed to hear, to release my pain and to be able to see the pain in everyone else.

The truth is that the information you get about another person can only help you to understand that person better and get an idea of what their pain is. The information they give you about **you** is what they can teach you about yourself. Daniel is consistently pushing me to look at myself. To think about my behavior and why I do the things I do.

I mean, look at my first marriage. I learned that I am **not** nothing and that everyone deserves to be loved just as they are. Discovering that I am good enough to be loved for who I am. Also realizing that you can't change others and that it is not your place to fix anyone else. You can only change yourself when you are ready to change. Please read that again: when you are **ready** to change.

Daniel has given me the best gift of all, and that is **me**. Finding my way back to me, and feeling that I am home. I have more to give; more time, more love, more **me**, because everything I have to give is inside of me.

Daniel said something to me recently that resonated with me. He stated that the three of us is what matters, Daniel, Laura and me. He said we matter. And that was that. We do matter. Every one of us matters. It is up to us to know this truth so that when others try to put you down because that's how they have always pushed your buttons, you don't need to react to them anymore.

We have spent our whole lives reacting. Hence, when you know the truth of who you are, you can begin to respond and add value to the conversation. Furthermore, you will be listening to what others are saying to you.

Do you make them feel like they have value in your life?

Do you make them feel insignificant?

Are they telling you that you are not expressing your love in a way that they understand?

Are they telling you that you are taking them for granted?

I can promise you; it is never about you. Rather, it is about how you make others feel. If you make others feel unappreciated or unwanted, it will be brought to your attention one way or another. Do you make other people feel unworthy of your love or beneath you like they are inferior? This is what the other person is trying to tell you. If you get offended, it is because you realize that you have been treating this individual unfairly. Therefore, change the way you deal with others, and you will feel better and so will they.

Pay attention, and you will begin to understand how others are telling you how they feel and what they need. However, if you feel offended or upset by what is said, it is because you still believe that you are unworthy and not good enough and you need to kick these old habits in the butt. Give them a good swift kick. Say goodbye to all the lies you have been telling yourself all these years. Finally, start embracing the truth of who you are.

Repeat these with me:

I am worthy of love just as I am.

I am good enough to be loved, just as I am.

Others deserve to receive my love.

There is an infinite amount of love in my heart for me to give away freely and it will never run out.

If you feel that you have done things that are unforgivable, you must forgive yourself first. Accept that you did the best you could do with the knowledge you had at the time. In each moment we are evolving, we are changing. All things considered, you now have all this new information. From here on, you have so many different ways that you can make peace with what has happened and move forward. Presently, I have given you many tools to set yourself free with this book.

Quit making excuses and stop being afraid. Your life is waiting for you. Every day it is calling you to fall in love with who you are. Furthermore, fall in love with your life and everything that is about you. Forget about what everyone else is doing, because that is **their** life. Also, forget about what you think you should be doing. Just breathe and look at yourself. Look at what you have created so far in your life because it is amazing. Most of all, look at all the people you have touched just by being alive.

If I'd have stayed in my first marriage, I could not have gained the insight I have gained with Daniel. My focus was completely on another person. That's what I understood love was. But I constantly tell my moms that come to lessons here, if you are always putting everyone else first and you run yourself into the ground trying to keep up, who will take care of your family?

If you are continually putting others first, you will never see what real love is. True love is inside of you, and as you are looking outwardly towards others, you cannot see the infinite amount of love that is already within you. Waiting for you to tap into it and give it the world.

My only wish is that one day I may give Daniel this amazing gift of being able to see himself through our eyes and therefore know how beautiful he truly is. We are all walking through this life unaware of how magnificent we are. We admire others when there is so much beauty and light within each of us.

All those qualities you so admire in other people are also inside of you. You have just decided somewhere along the line that you are not these things, but you have the same capacity.

If you've had any relationships with partners in your life, I urge you to sit down quietly right now and look at what they have contributed to you. What have you learned about yourself from these relationships? What have they taught you about yourself?

Each moment is a gift to you that you may know who you are. Sometimes relationships bring out the worst in us. They show us what we are capable of doing. We may not be proud of who we are when we share our lives with these partners, but give thanks. Be grateful. It is all there for you.

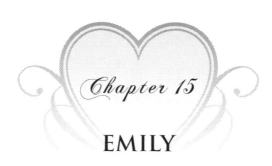

Chapter 15

EMILY

This woman is also incredibly resilient. She is amazing. For years, I borrowed money from Emily, and one way or another something would happen that I couldn't pay her back. Just like Sarah at the office, she never once said no. She always helped me.

For the longest time, I thought I could never repay her all the money she had lent me over the years, but then something changed inside of me. I was able to give her the most wonderful gift. The gift of her knowing how amazing she is. How truly beautiful she is and how strong she has always been. Letting her see how incredibly valuable she is to us.

She also gives me so much insight every single day through our conversations. We are always learning from each other and from sharing our experiences. My insight on money and the clarity with which I see this subject now has been thanks to her.

She never said anything or made me feel guilty. Emily was always happy to lend me cash, even though she could perceive that I felt awful every time I needed to borrow it. She has endured hours of me asking her questions. Never having any answers, because the answers were always inside of me. I was always waiting for her to say something insightful and full of wisdom, but the listening was all that was needed.

Spending months asking her, "Why am I infuriated all the time and why is there always this need to feel resentment towards someone?" Then there was the most important of all questions. "Now that Laura is here, why aren't I blissfully happy?"

She has been kind enough to share her stories with me, and these have helped me to understand my mom better but also myself. I have learned so much about myself from her stories and her experiences. It is astonishing how much we all have in common.

In this chapter, I wanted to talk about judgment. It is so easy to judge others when we don't know the truth about them. Some people are too ashamed of who they are for you to get to know them at all. Studying the self-esteem course with Emily, many things have come to the surface for both of us.

When I was growing up, directly across from us, lived a couple called John and Elizabeth. They were an elderly couple both with gray and white hair. Elizabeth had been born in Australia, and just like me, her parents were also from Argentina, so she knew how to speak Spanish very well. This couple didn't have any children of their own, and they adopted us as their grandchildren. Mom would often go over to help them with their gardening.

Elizabeth was very kind and very soft spoken. John kept to himself. He was always very cranky and moody. Despite being so different, they had been married for over fifty years. Elizabeth taught me how to crochet and knit. She was very talented with her hands. Often we could hear John yelling at Elizabeth from our house. I always loved Elizabeth as if she were our very own grandmother. John passed away shortly after I turned fourteen.

My parents came home from the funeral talking about a strange man that had appeared to pay his respects. Nobody knew who he was. After I had returned to Australia for the last time, I visited Elizabeth just before she died. I had always kept in touch with her. She told me that many years later that strange man came to her house and they eventually became very close friends. With time he confessed to her that he had been John's lover. John and his partner were in love for over forty years, but they were too scared to live a life together because of how society dealt with Gay men.

I always remember this couple when I think about judging something. We never really know what is going on with other people. Not even with your partner. You may believe that you are in love and that they are the love of your life, but you can never truly know what they are thinking or feeling. Many people live in pain. They are too afraid to live the life that would make their heart sing. Too many of us, worry about what others think. What they might say about us.

It is so easy to pass judgment on others. We never knew why John was so reserved or why he yelled at Elizabeth. Mom couldn't understand why Elizabeth didn't just leave him? Why did she put up with his abusive behavior? I guess, after many years of the same treatment, this way of life becomes routine. Perhaps, Elizabeth had grown up treated even worse as a child, and to her, John was gentle in comparison. Maybe her father had been horrible to her. Who knows?

Sometimes, no matter how unkind others are, we can't help but love them. We recognize something in them that they can't see in themselves. The few times John did interact with us, he was funny and smart. We loved listening to his stories even though this didn't happen very often. Sometimes he gifted us with his music by playing the violin beautifully.

We learn to judge from such an early age. Our parents are

continually criticizing others in front of us. Telling us this is bad and that is unacceptable behavior. Judgment makes us look outside of ourselves. It makes us put labels on others. While we are focusing on others, we don't have time to look at our issues.

Are you going to spend the rest of your life in self-loathing? Not being able to be yourself and never fitting in. The truth is that there are others out there just like you. No matter what your situation is. Seek out their help or hold out your hand to help others with the same issues as you. You'll be surprised at just how many will show up. Nobody wants to be alone in their pain.

It is easy to judge others and many times we judge others as harshly as we judge ourselves. While we are judging, we are not accepting. Accept that there is probably a reason why that person is that way. Nobody is born cruel or mean. We become that way from our experiences. Also, start to observe your behavior. How often are you unkind to others due to your frustrations? You are rude and short tempered at others because you are preoccupied with your concerns.

When you can start to see this within you, then you can begin to recognize it in everyone. As a result, you will see the pain behind every unkind deed and word. Nothing is random. Nothing is without cause.

MY DAUGHTER

This angel entering my life has been a complete blessing. Every day she teaches me something new, for example: that we had everything we needed when we were born. Joy, love, sadness, life. The simplicity of it all is overwhelming, and yet we have managed to over-complicate everything. I feel that I learn more from her than I could ever teach her. She teaches me about patience and tolerance, not to mention what love really is.

She shows me what self-love looks like every day too. Laura is the reason I strive to be better and better every single day. Not just in a financial way, but as a human being. It is my job to set the example for her that she may know what matters in life, knowing that she matters to God and to us and most importantly that we will always be with her. Hopefully she will never feel lonely because we are never really alone. It is our perception of life that makes us feel that way.

Laura will learn that we are all connected and that everything we do affects others. So we need to be mindful of the words we speak and the intention with which we set forth our actions towards others. Everything comes back to us. Every kindness and every cruel act.

In her first three years of life, Laura was completely

self-absorbed. Everything was about discovering and exploring. Even with her voice. She would spend days exploring the sounds that she could produce. Looking at the world as if everything was new to her and it was. She was seeing the world for the first time, but she showed me how to look at things as if for the first time because I had forgotten how to do this. In reality, we *are* looking at it for the first time.

Every time you look at something, you are looking at it for the first time because you are a different person in every moment. We are always evolving and assimilating this amazing thing called life. Not only that, but you haven't looked at that particular thing before, whether it be a butterfly or a cat or the moon. The sky never looks the same either. Everything is constantly changing.

All of a sudden, spiders no longer look the same. Laura is obsessed with their intricate webs, and I have started to take more notice of the detail in their design. It is amazing. She is also fascinated with pretty much every bug she sees. Moths, butterflies, beetles. I realize that I have never actually looked at the world as an adult. We take it all for granted and decide that it's not important. We stop looking at it because we have already seen it many times before. But this is where the miracles are. Every time we witness life in any form, this is a miracle.

Whenever Daniel and I are discussing a difference in opinions, and the conversation can get a little heated sometimes, Laura always tells us to stop it. She knows when we are fighting and when we are loving. She knows the difference, and is only four years old! When did we decide that it is okay to argue and feel bad most of the time, even a four-year-old knows that this is not the way? When she was younger, she would cry and scream because she didn't know another way to express this change in energy. It made her uncomfortable enough to step in and tell us in her way, that there is a better way.

We need to stop resisting change and flow with it. Allow it to affect you and grow as a human being. If it does not serve you, then you discard it. Let go of everything that makes you feel bad. There is no reason to hold onto them anymore.

Here is another example of how our children teach us. My cousin, Sofia has been telling her six-year-old daughter, Ellie, how gorgeous she is since she was born. I was doing the same with Laura because as I mentioned earlier, our parents never told us, how gorgeous we were. One morning Ellie said to her: "Mummy, you are so beautiful and I am so ugly."

This observation got me thinking. We are telling our children how beautiful they are with **words**, all the while **feeling** ugly inside ourselves. Her daughter was merely voicing what my cousin was saying to her all those years. You, my darling are the most beautiful thing I have ever seen, but I feel unattractive. Isn't that incredible? She is just six years old! Our children are always teaching us if we would but listen.

Speaking of beauty, when Laura was born, people would tell me that I looked like her. I would look at her and think to myself are we even looking at the same thing? After the second year, people kept telling me that she looked so much like me. I thought she was the most beautiful thing I had ever seen. How could I possibly look like her? I would always say "thank you" for the compliment, but in my mind, I couldn't help but think, "Are you blind?"

I'm ugly, and she is gorgeous. She is an angel. How could I possibly look anything like that? As more people told me that she was gorgeous and that she looked like me, I started thinking that my perception of myself was warped. Something ugly cannot create something beautiful I began to think to myself every day until one day, I looked in the mirror, and I could see Laura in me.

I have always been attractive. I just didn't know it. This has been the hardest thing for me to accept about myself. Saying "I love you" to myself was much easier than saying "I am beautiful." I find the beauty in others so effortlessly and yet there is so much resistance when I try to see my own.

We think it is our job to teach our children. I believe they are here to remind us of who we are. They remind us to slow down, and they tell us to look at ourselves all the time. Looking at themselves in the mirror every chance they get. Children know that they are a gift to the world. They know how magnificent they are. We are the ones who have forgotten. And so every day, I try to observe and learn what she can teach me on this particular day.

The last few days she keeps asking me: "Mom, are you loving?" and "Mom are you happy?" I don't know where she learned this? I believe it is a reminder from up above. When I asked Grandma, she had no clue where she heard that. She wasn't going to preschool or daycare at the time. Where she got that from is a mystery to me. I just give thanks every day that she is reminding me that this is the reason we are here.

I haven't stopped yelling yet when I get frustrated with her, but I understand that it is not necessary and it doesn't accomplish anything. If I don't like something, I can just change it because I have that power. I have always had that power. I need to remind myself every day that she does not think the same way that we think as adults because her brain hasn't finished forming. Some parts are incomplete. When she interrupts me and can't wait for me to listen to her, it has to do with her forgetting what she was going to say. She doesn't understand what interrupting means.

Laura also shows me how I have no control over anything and that is okay. I can't control her, and it is not my job. Just as

I can't control Daniel, or his mom or my parents, or the weather. We are not here to control anything. Wanting to control things and people around us is an act of fear and not of love.

I wanted to include this because so many parents feel that they need to control their kids. Either to keep them safe or to make sure they fit in at school and in society. Meanwhile, you need to understand that we are not supposed to be the same as anyone else and that it is okay to be uniquely you. Only then will you know that there is nothing to do but love life just as it is. Embrace who you are. From here on, accept who you are, just as you are.

I spent years not brushing my teeth. The good part of a decade. I hated my teeth so much for all the pain I had suffered at the dentists because of them. They are not in good shape at the moment, but I understand that I have done this with my attitude towards myself. If there is any part of you that you are not loving, it will suffer. It will let you know that you do not love yourself. I know this for a fact.

There is the beauty of it. Your body and those around you are letting you know at all times, whether you love yourself or not. There is never any doubt. Just look at yourself. Does your body feel energetic? Is it healthy and full of energy? Are there any parts that are in pain? Look at the people around you. Are they loving and kind or are they angry and frustrating to you?

Start observing what is around you more carefully, because it is all there for you. It is always telling you how you are feeling about yourself and what you believe about yourself. Therefore, pay attention to what you are attracting into your life.

Television, magazines and the media keep bombarding us with what beautiful looks like. You have to ask yourself, though, who decided that what is in the magazines and on television is what beautiful looks like. They teach us that beauty is external and that we can be just as beautiful as what we see in the media if we purchase their products to look like them.

Another concept I don't understand is when people go on about being the same. "The same as who?" is always my question. If we were meant to be, all the same, we would all be doctors or teachers or astronauts. We would all enjoy eating the same food. We don't all like the same things. Some of us love reading books while others love painting and creating music.

I get confused when parents talk about their children being bullied because they are different. We should be focusing our energy on the child who doesn't want to be unique and cheering on the kid that embraces his individuality. Stand out of the crowd. Be yourself. Be unique. If we were meant to be the same, we would all have the same hair color, eye color, fingerprints, and desires. Why do we follow the herd when all the evidence tells us that we are supposed to be different?

I am writing these thoughts to challenge you today. Look at your thoughts and look at your beliefs. You need to question everything you have been told especially about yourself. Ask yourself, "Does it serve me?" Remember this means, does this make me feel good?

Does it serve you to think that you are ugly, stupid, fat, or not good enough in any way? Similarly, does it help to think that you can't do certain things? Does it feel nice to believe that you're unwanted, invisible or not worthy of love? Then why do you keep doing that? **Stop it right now!**

At this point in your life, it is imperative to reassess how you have been talking to yourself. You were not put here on this earth to feel dreadful 24/7. In fact, it is quite the opposite. We are ultimately here to experience life. To know ourselves through the experiences that we have.

At the end of the day, *you* are the only one that lives in your head. Deciding what to believe and what thoughts reside there. Consistently choosing the thoughts that are repeating over and over and over again in your mind. Look at your life. Are you happy with your life as it is at this very moment? Does it feel like something is missing or not quite, right? This feeling is the reason you are here reading this book. Just like me, you are looking for answers.

Be honest with yourself and look at what you think about most of the time. Can you look at yourself in the mirror and think "I like myself, just as I am." I am amazing. I love being me?" All things considered, this is your life!

In the meantime, others aren't allowed in because it's impossible to love the person you look at every day in the mirror. There is a part of yourself that you are rejecting, and this keeps people at a distance, never allowing them to get close. Regrettably, until you can accept every single part of your being, you won't be able to love others completely or allow them to love you exactly as you are. So it is essential to start right there. Figure out what it is that you are rejecting about yourself. Look at the truth in it. Start looking at all the positive things you are and build from there.

Chapter 17

THOUGHTS TODAY

Now let's talk about anger and being angry all the time. When we are angry, we are focusing on others. On what they have done wrong. We are not looking at ourselves and how we have created this situation. We are not taking responsibility for the things we don't like in our lives. Constantly blaming others because it is too painful to look at who we are and what we have done. It is too painful to accept that we believe we are unlovable, unworthy, or not good enough. Not measuring up hurts too much, so we judge others. We make them wrong and focus all our energy on them.

The only way to understand is to get to the root of it all. In my case, the moment my sister came into the world, I decided that I was unwanted and unlovable. The moment I believed that I was not worthy of love was the moment my anger was born. This whole process began two years ago and is still a work in progress. I am still discovering things about myself, but am now in love with the process and can't stop. Learning more about myself, makes me want to know more.

Not looking at ourselves takes me to another subject: judgment. When we judge something, we put it in a place of wrongness. We need to understand that everything has its place. I used to judge my mother for yelling at me and spanking me, yet here I was yelling at my three-year-old and watching her react the way I used to, when I was her age. Without my experience of it as a mother, I could never understand my mom's frustration, my mom's anger. I am not condoning the action. Everything is there for a reason. It helped me realize that the yelling was never about me. It was always about her, just as my shouting was about me feeling inadequate and not about what Laura had done.

Now here is an interesting topic regarding judgment. I am completely against spanking. I don't see the value of it at all or that I learned anything from it as a child, yet so many parents do it. I have come to understand that these parents are doing it out of love. They believe that if the child doesn't follow their rules, these kids won't fit into society and will be outcast. Their children will be bullied or mocked by others. They believe that they are doing what is best for that child, so that they won't suffer out in the real world.

Somehow from very young, I knew that I was different and I was so happy not to be the same as anyone else. Apart from my Dad, there wasn't anyone that I admired enough to want to be like them. I enjoyed being me too much. Living in the moment and not having to worry about anything. Learning was easy for me, and sports was so much fun. Life was excellent.

I know what it feels like to be so far from love that you want to hurt everyone and everything so that they know exactly how much you hurt inside. Words cannot explain this pain, but it has been my greatest gift. Without it, I could never understand how people are unkind to others. It hurts when people are kind to you. Everything hurts. You just want the world to go away and leave you alone.

Some of my life chapters may sound "negative." They were necessary to get me to this point in my life. What I've learned is that in the worst moments in my life, the moments of the most suffering, my thoughts, and my feelings were negative. By negative, I mean, thoughts of fear, thoughts of lack, thoughts of being separate, thoughts that made me feel awful inside about myself. Thoughts of joy and thoughts of love created very different experiences in my life. So I know that your thoughts and your feelings create your reality. It is impossible to have bad thoughts and feel good.

You can't think that you are fat and stupid and feel good about yourself. The same way you can't believe you are intelligent and beautiful and an amazing human being with so much to contribute to the world and feel bad about yourself. Your thoughts are a guide as to what you are feeling, just as your feelings are guiding you as to what you are thinking.

Look carefully at what you are thinking throughout the day, especially, if you are feeling angry, frustrated and annoyed most of the time. In your mind, some thoughts are repeatedly replaying over and over again. Write these down and look at them carefully. You know, for a long time, I was the loudest person in the room. Granted, my whole family is loud, but I realize that the reason for this behavior was that I didn't want to be invisible anymore. I was now screaming to be the center of attention.

I believe with all my heart that until you can open your eyes and truly see your personal history and find the gifts in every event that has affected you, you will continue to react to life. You will continue to repeat your patterns that you have already set in motion. Holding on to misinterpretations about others, but most importantly, holding on to delusions about yourself. You believe things that are not true about who you are. Over time you have made things up about yourself, and you have spent a lifetime collecting evidence to prove your theories about who you are in the world.

I know that it's hard, but please I urge you to go back and read the chapters again. Complete the exercises. Memories will come to the surface that need healing. Once you've healed these, more will come to the surface for healing. Fall in love with your life. Fall in love with who you are. You need to analyze everything that was passed down by your parents, your teachers, relatives, any adults that tried to teach you something as you were growing up. Question everything. For the most part, adults are just passing on their "knowledge," their insecurities, their beliefs, their experiences. Just because an adult said it, doesn't mean that it is the truth.

There's a very simple way to work out if something is true or not. Ask yourself, then notice how you feel. For example, in my case, every time I thought I was separate from God, this made me feel sad. The truth fills your heart with love and joy. Knowing that my Dad has always loved me, makes me feel overjoyed even to this day. Thinking that my mom didn't want me infuriated me.

Change starts with you. You have to make the decision today if something doesn't serve you, in other words, if it makes you feel bad, then you will take steps to change it. Work out where your triggers originated from in your past. For example, for me, my primary trigger was that my mom cast me aside and didn't love me anymore. When I understood that this could not possibly be true, then I got rid of that trigger.

All the things we hold onto from our past create buttons. People show up in our lives to push these buttons. They tell us that we believe things about ourselves that are not true. They are there to remind you that you do not love some part of yourself. You are not accepting something about yourself.

With judgment comes resistance. I will try to explain this as simply as possible because, for the longest time, I couldn't understand this concept. When you judge something, you decide that it is wrong. For example, when I had been taught for all those years through the church and my parents, that having money was evil and only corrupt people are wealthy. So I kept pushing money away only allowing a small amount to come in. Resisting it and not letting it come to me because I had judged it as something wrong.

I like to think of God as my parent. Parents take care of you until you are old enough to take care of yourself, then they have to let you go so you can live your life. Make your choices, create your experiences. I started talking to Him again after Laura was born when I realized that we are not separate beings and that He doesn't judge anything I do. He looks at me as His child, the same way I look at Laura.

He is constantly talking to me, sending me signs and letting me know He is there, just as our parents are there when we feel like talking to them. We pick up the phone and have a chat, and we feel better that we spoke to them. I always refer to God as He or Him because it doesn't matter. He doesn't have a gender but to create life, we need both male and female. We cannot create human life without both sexes. The egg needs the sperm to germinate.

As God is in all things, I can communicate with Him all the time if I wish to. Sometimes I see Him in my daughter's smile, in the twinkle of her eyes when she is cheeky, in my dog's beautiful, warm, loving eyes or even in just a gorgeous sunset. I give thanks that He is in all these things and that He created them all for me to enjoy.

What would be the point of giving us free will if He was going to judge everything we did? That makes no sense at all. Creation is creation. It is not right or wrong, it just is. What we do with our bodies, what we do to others, are all expressions of who we are inside. When you are in love with your life and with who you are, others will be blessed to cross your path.

Your love will radiate towards them and lift them up and warm their souls.

If you are in pain and hurting, your presence still blesses others. It gives people an opportunity to express love and compassion towards you, or it gives them a chance to express their anger and pain. Either way, everything is a blessing. Everything is an opportunity for you to *be* who you want to *be*.

When humans are cruel to animals, we focus on the cruelty and the heartless person committing the barbaric act. The truth is that this has created an opportunity for others to express their kindness and their compassion towards these living creatures. Everything has its place in this universe. The same happens with abused people. We focus on the attacker, but this has created an opportunity for people to show love and compassion for the person that was hurt. It also creates an opening for the attacker to receive sympathy and understanding.

We tend to forget that the attacker was once the victim. Being abused themselves, they now pass on the torment that was inflicted upon them. Attackers view the world as normal. Hurting others on a daily basis is normal. Living in pain is common behavior. They do not know that there is a whole world out there that does not live this way. An entire world who doesn't think that this way of life is ordinary at all.

When we understand that people who hurt others are in the most self-loathing and suffering, then we can move forward to becoming a better world. We need to help others know that they are worthy of love. They always have been. We all are. Love is all there is.

I find it curious that we can have one parent that is unconditional love, just absolutely loves you exactly how you are. While the other parent has trouble expressing the same love, and we focus on this parent. We concentrate on the fact that they withdraw their love as a punishment when we don't do what they want us to do. As a result, we start to think that there is something wrong with us.

We work hard to earn this parent's love all the time, but no matter how hard we try it is never good enough, assuming all the time that we are at fault and not the other way around. Needing to be something else for that parent to approve of us entirely and so the quest begins. We spend our lives doing this and trying that, only to realize that it will never be enough. I am starting to believe that this is the way it's designed. Thinking we are not good enough, is how the ego is born.

This parent doesn't know how to receive love from something so innocent and pure. They see you in your natural state when you are born. Being pure love and pure joy, and they feel that they don't deserve having you in their lives. When Laura was born, I kept thinking that I didn't deserve to have something so beautiful and so precious in my care. It was never about you, my dear soul. You were absolute perfection and did you want to know a secret? You still are!

No matter what has happened to you in your life. No matter what you have done to others, the moment you realize **who** you are at this moment, your life will never be the same. It can't be. You are no longer holding on to all those lies that you have believed about yourself.

When you don't think that you deserve something, you push it away. It is just a natural reaction. You have spent years deciding that you don't deserve to feel good about yourself that you don't know another **way to be**, but I am telling you now, there is another way to live.

Here I wanted to address the issue of wanting to control others. What do we accomplish with this? Does it make us feel that we have power over others? You can never have complete control over another person because you can never fully know what is going on in their head. Look at this carefully. Again, if you are trying to control someone else, then you are focusing on another person and not yourself.

Regularly telling that person that they are not good enough as they are. If you don't do what I want you to do, then I will retract my love and show my disapproval for you. Therefore teaching others that they need to do certain things to **earn** your love. You do not give your love freely. It is not unconditional. My Mom's love felt this way.

I always sensed that I had to earn her love. Working hard for it or she wouldn't love me. I had to be a "good" girl for her to accept me. Mistakes were bad. I couldn't make mistakes. Otherwise she would punish me for them. How do we learn if we can't make mistakes? Who is to decide how many times you need to do something before you learn from it?

As an example, look at me with money. I spent years borrowing from Emily then felt terrible that I couldn't pay her back. While I now understand the reason behind this, for a very long time, the same mistake was repeated many, many, many, many times before noticing my pattern and more importantly, understanding that I didn't need to do that anymore. Emily was kind enough to have the patience to let me do it as much as I needed until I was ready to wake up to myself.

Here I'd like to discuss when adults speak of respect. They are talking about fear. They are saying that if the child "respects" them that the child will do what they ask. But the truth is that many times, this child acts from fear. They are afraid of the punishment that will come if they don't do what adults expect of them. Being afraid of the consequences is not respect. Children copy everything adults do. So if you are unkind to animals or rude to other people, your kids will do exactly that.

Try to understand that everything your infant is going through is a phase and has nothing to do with you. When they are going through their "no" phase, they are not trying to be difficult. They are testing out their power of the little they have control over in the world. Saying "no" to everything is a natural phase, and all toddlers go through it. We see it as defiance, which is an adult trait. Again, we take on everything as an attack towards us. Rather than try to understand that this is necessary for the child's development.

I believe that children go through this phase because they are constantly having to listen to us and follow our rules. So at some stage, they decide that they have that same power. They have the same right, that when they say something that others will listen to them. How funny is it that we naturally go through this phase at the age of three, then we forget and spend the rest of our lives in conflict saying yes when we don't want to do things?

Even three-year-olds know how it works, but we insist on telling them not to do what is natural to all of us: saying **no** when we don't want to do something, or we simply don't want something.

Also, how confusing is it to a child when parents swear and then reprimand their children for swearing? They are training the children to do as I say, but not as I do. They are teaching double standards, and the truth is that they are worried that their children will cuss out in public and embarrass them. I know because my Dad used to swear a lot and my Mom was always telling us not to say those words that they were inappropriate.

Controlling others is our way of not wanting to look within. Not wanting to accept the moment in time that we decided that we weren't good enough for someone else's love. Refusing to recognize the moment in time that we decided we were unlovable and unworthy of love. You have always been loved, and the person that is craving your love more than anyone else in the world is *you*. Your spirit wants to know that you acknowledge how amazing you truly are. I call it spirit, but you can call it whatever you want.

It is that thing inside that has thought. That thing inside all of us that feels. It's telling you what to believe and what to decide is important in every moment. That thing inside us that protects us from pain and yearns to feel loved and cherished. Comprehending how magnificent you are and how much you deserve to be loved, will allow others a place in your life. You will keep pushing others away and not let them in because you feel unattractive and unlovable.

Another way to get an idea of where we are in our lives is to observe how we treat our possessions, material belongings, and other people. How you treat your car, the house or any material object screams mountains about how you feel about yourself and how you treat others even more so. Do you take care of your belongings?

For the longest time, I handled my car like it was junk. I managed my house the same way. I saw nothing to be grateful for in either of these things, but just the mere fact that I felt this way about them was telling me that I thought I was junk. In other words, not worth looking after. Not worth cleaning or maintaining it. Not worth giving it any love at all. The only reason they would cross my mind were if they broke down, and that was only because it was an inconvenience to me. The same with my body. When my body got sick, I would get frustrated with it for not functioning properly, but I never gave it any love.

It was when we bought a car that we both fell in love with that things started to change. Now, you won't believe this story. Our cars have been hit three times by other drivers in the past ten years, while we were stationary in a parking spot. All three times, the person that hit our car left a note with their details taking responsibility for the repairs, and they paid for them.

Three times! That's amazing, right? It never cost us a cent to have them fixed. Now that is the power of love.

Are you kind to others or do you treat them like they are not worth your time? Do you treat others with love and respect or do you treat them like they are worthless, useless and beneath you? Saying someone is beneath you is the same as saying they are better than you. You are trying to prove that you are smarter or better than others in some way because deep down inside you don't feel that you are. Otherwise, there would be no need to put others down. Feeling superior or feeling inferior to others just states that you are not accepting yourself and you are not accepting of others the way they are.

If you are always putting yourself down, criticizing yourself and belittling yourself that you are not good enough, that you don't measure up, what chance does anyone else stand? You are going to measure everyone with the same ruler.

One thing you can do today to change your life is to shift your focus. Instead of focusing on why someone doesn't love you, think of someone you can give your love to today. You have an infinite amount of love to give. Don't worry about being rejected. Love is not about being accepted or knocked back. Love wants to be given away freely, no strings attached, like the wind or like the sun that rises every morning and provides its warmth and its light. The sun never says that you owe it anything. The sun gives you its love every day.

It is never about what you get back when you love; it is all about giving to another because you have it to give. Most of us have grown up with the mentality "what's in it for me?" When you love, you become alive. Your life takes flight. You never look at the world the same way again. When that light switch (as I like to call it), goes off in your mind, you will become unstoppable.

Life is about you taking responsibility for every word and

every action that comes from you. It was never about others. They are each looking for their way out of the maze. Understand that everything that you put out is a reflection of how you feel about yourself. This is the biggest realization of them all.

For a time, I treated Daniel like he didn't matter. I treated him like he was unwanted because that is how I felt inside. He would come home, and I wouldn't even say hello or ask him how his day was. I was the same with Emily. Treating her like I didn't care. Like she didn't matter. I was simply using her to keep my debt addiction going. I had no regard for how they were feeling or how I made them feel. The only thing I was sure of, was how I felt. Because at the end of the day, that's all that matters to anyone. We only care about how we each feel individually.

The most important thing to understand is that we are kind to others because it makes us feel good to be kind. Therefore we are unkind to others when we don't feel good about ourselves inside. Everything is a reflection of what we are feeling inside. You cannot feel good about who you are and want to make others feel bad about themselves.

Many years just rolled into each other. Each year felt like the year before. I felt like I was on a hamster wheel just regurgitating the same year over and over again. This went on for at least fifteen years. Nothing changing. Nothing getting better. Everything just flew past in a blur. We hadn't finished one Christmas when the next one was upon us.

I lived every moment worried about the future. How was I going to pay the bills? About the lack of money. Where could I get more money? What could I do to bring in more? I didn't know what gratitude was or how to just be in the moment because to be in the moment you have to be comfortable with who you are. If you are thinking about the future, you don't have to be present to who you are right now at this moment.

I spent many sleepless nights worrying about how to pay for everything, rather than looking for a solution to the problem. You become so involved in the problem that you complain about how bad it is instead of looking how to fix it. Believing that this is your lot in life, that this is what you deserve, and nothing will ever improve.

The only time I would be fully present was in my piano lessons because I thought that I owed my students at least that much. Giving them my undivided attention and making them feel important. Making them feel that they mattered.

Now you know there is a way out. Work through it. Find your way. Find the solutions to your problems. Everything is fixable. Nothing is beyond repair. It only is if you believe that it is. Stop making excuses and start living your life today. Do what makes you happy and know that you deserve to be happy. We all do.

I promise you that it has nothing to do with money and nothing to do with anyone else. The answers are all inside of you, and if you have been following my exercises carefully and been completely honest with yourself, some of the answers have already started to surface for you.

We are born with everything we need to live a happy life. Then we have grown-ups telling us that we need to be this to be accepted and we need to be that to fit in and be loved by others. Some of us have grown-ups that hurt us and make us believe that we don't deserve love and we don't deserve to be happy. But the truth is that they are your birthright.

The more I look at life, the more I realize that it is just like piano lessons. When students come, they have their natural way of playing. Some play smooth and connect all the notes. We call this legato in music. Others play all the notes bouncy and separate. We call this staccato. The ones that start off legato need to learn how to play staccato and vice versa.

Once they gain this skill, then they get to do different things with each hand. Maybe the first year, they learn to play one hand staccato, while the other does legato. The following year they master playing dynamics, this means that they play the keys softly or loudly to make a range of different sounds within the same notes. Then they must be able to play one hand louder than the other. Otherwise, you can't hear the melody (the part that you can sing). Don't get me started on crossing one hand over the other.

In life, we are born with our natural skills. We may be naturally patient, and we may be good listeners, but perhaps we are not compassionate towards others. We may be kind and honest but not empathetic towards the needs of others. As we go through each year, life keeps throwing people, circumstances, and events at us to give us the opportunity to gain new skills as human beings. We can learn to become better listeners. We can learn to be more generous with our time and our hearts.

The truth is we are all here to keep gaining skills and hence knowing who we are. Knowing that we are love and patience. Knowing that we are giving and kind and loyal. One thing is to know the word and understand what it means. Another is to know ourselves as these things because we have experienced ourselves **being** them.

I know I said that we were meant to be different. We challenge each other to look at things differently so we can gain these new skills. At the end of the day, we all bleed the same color blood regardless of the color of our skin, and we all breathe the same air to live. Everyone eats food and drinks water to survive. We all want the same thing: to know that we matter. Feeling loved and being able to give our love, is the reason we exist.

We want to express our love so that we may know that we are love. Every single person on this Earth without exception. Without love, we would cease to exist. Love is what makes two people come together and want to create a new life. Either the adult wants to feel loved by the other adult, or they wish to give their love to their offspring. If we didn't feel the need to be loved or to give our love, we would no longer need others, and life would cease to exist. This is the beauty of life.

This has been my story. What's yours?

YOUR LIFE

0-5 years.

Here you need to write down every single memory you can recall of the first five years of your life. Just write the event as it happened, without any interpretation of it.

_____

_____

_____

_____

_____

_____

_____

_____

_____

_____

_____

_____

_____

In this section, you need to write down all of the thoughts that you can recollect about each of the memories you wrote down above.

_____

_____

_____

_____

_____

_____

_____

_____

_____

_____

_____

_____

_____

_____

_____

_____

_____

_____

_____

_____

_____

Now, use this section to write down how many of the above were facts and how many were interpretations. Make notes on your thoughts as to whether they are interpretations that serve you, or do they make you feel bad about who you are.

5-10 years.

Write down every memory you can recall between the age of five and ten years old. Remember, to just write down the facts.

_____

_____

_____

_____

_____

_____

_____

_____

_____

_____

_____

_____

_____

_____

_____

_____

_____

_____

_____

Here, you can write down every thought regarding each memory above.

Again, look at how many of these interpretations were made up in your head and do not serve you today.

10-15 years.

Write down all the memories you have of this period of your life.
Write down what actually happened.

_____

_____

_____

_____

_____

_____

_____

_____

_____

_____

_____

_____

_____

_____

_____

_____

_____

_____

_____

_____

_____

_____

_____

Here you can write down your thoughts and feelings about each of the memories you remembered above.

How many of these are interpretations that do not serve you?
How many of these thoughts make you feel bad about who you
are today?

15-20 years.

Write down all the events that occurred in these five years of your life. Especially regarding the relationships you have developed at this stage.

_____

_____

_____

_____

_____

_____

_____

_____

_____

_____

_____

_____

_____

_____

_____

_____

_____

_____

_____

_____

Write down all your thoughts. What you were thinking about yourself and what you thought about others.

How many of these interpretations make you feel good about who you are today? Are any of these interpretations still true today? Can you let any of them go?

20+ years.

Continue the process we began above. Break your life into five year intervals and keep making notes of the facts and then make sure to look at how you interpreted these events.

The interpretations that are made up in your head and don't make you feel good about the person you are today are thoughts that you can slowly start to release.

Give thanks for every single one of them because they have made you who you are at this very moment. Anything you don't like, you can change. You have the power to do that. You have always had the ability to do that.

You may wish to buy a journal for this section of the book. I doubt that you will have enough space to write down all your memories here. This is your life. Fall in love with it. Fall in love with who you truly are.

_____

_____

_____

_____

_____

_____

_____

_____

_____

_____

ABOUT THE AUTHOR

Hollie Belle lives with her daughter and husband in Sydney, Australia. She has spent most of her life living in a fog. Hollie has always known that she is different and unique. Since her awakening, she is passionate about sharing her knowledge with everyone that is ready to hear it. Her intention is to help others gain clarity about their own lives and help them find their true purpose in life. Hollie has spent the last forty years looking for answers to life's most important questions. Her quest is now to shed some light on these for others.

She enjoys playing piano, spending time with her family and goofing around with her dog called Mike. Hollie finds that the most challenging part of writing is the frequent interruptions from her daughter, but knows that once it is finally published, it will all be worth it. This book started off as a gift for Hollie's loved ones, but she soon discovered that this needed to be made available to everyone. The wisdom contained within these pages is for all human beings. Changing lives is her most heartfelt desire in life now.

Visit us at
www.yourpastisagift.com

You can also visit our Blog
www.easymindeasylife.com

Subscribe to the videos on our YouTube Channel:
www.youtube.com/c/easymindeasylife

This book is also available in EBook format.

USEFUL RESOURCES

You may want to try some of these out for yourself. Have fun!

Natural Healer - Melissa Crowhurst
www.naturalhealer.com.au

Easy Mind Easy Life - Hollie Belle
www.facebook.com/easymindeasylife

Infinity Light and Sound - Rafail Karivalis
https://www.facebook.com/groups/infinitylight8sound

Adventure in Oneness - Rikka Zimmerman
www.adventureinoneness.com

Life Changing Energy - Vickie Gould
www.lifechangingenergy.com

Natural Health News
https://www.youtube.com/@naturalhealthnews

Printed in the United States
by Baker & Taylor Publisher Services